Christmas

Recipes

Hannie P. Scott

www.HanniePScott.com

www.Hanniepscott.com

ISBN: 9781973386834

MY FREE GIFT TO YOU!

55

Quick
&
Easy
Recipes

hannie p. scott

To download your free gift, simply visit:

www.hanniepscott.com/freegift

TABLE OF CONTENTS

For more books by Hannie, please visit:
www.Hanniepscott.com/books

ABBREVIATIONS

oz = ounce

fl oz = fluid ounce

tsp = teaspoon

tbsp = tablespoon

ml = milliliter

c = cup

pt = pint

qt = quart

gal = gallon

L = liter

CONVERSIONS

1/2 fl oz = 3 tsp = 1 tbsp = 15 ml

1 fl oz = 2 tbsp = 1/8 c = 30 ml

2 fl oz = 4 tbsp = 1/4 c = 60 ml

4 fl oz = 8 tbsp = 1/2 c = 118 ml

8 fl oz = 16 tbsp = 1 c = 236 ml

16 fl oz = 1 pt = 1/2 qt = 2 c = 473 ml

128 fl oz = 8 pt = 4 qt = 1 gal = 3.78 L

BREAKFASTS

cranberry Apple Butter

Servings: 10-12

What you need:

- 16-20 apples; peeled, cored, and sliced
- 12-oz fresh cranberries
- 3 3/4 cups sugar
- 1 tbsp cinnamon
- 1/4 tsp cloves
- 6-8 pint jars (depending on how big your slow cooker is)

What to do:

1. Put the cranberries and apples in your slow cooker and turn your slow cooker on high.
2. Cook for 18 hours.
3. Add the sugar, cinnamon, and cloves. Stir well and cook for another 4 hours.
4. Spoon the apple butter into the jars, screw on the lids and rings, and let them cool on the counter.

Blueberry Breakfast Cake

Servings: 10

What you need:

- 1 stick butter, at room temperature
- 2 tsp lemon zest
- 1 cup of sugar
- 1 egg
- 1 tsp vanilla
- 2 cups flour
- 2 tsp baking powder
- 1 tsp salt
- 2 cups fresh blueberries
- 1/2 cup buttermilk
- 1 tbsp sugar

What to do:

1. Preheat your oven to 350 degrees F.
2. With an electric mixer, cream together the butter, lemon zest, and 1 cup of sugar until light and fluffy.
3. Add the egg and vanilla and beat until combined.
4. Whisk together the flour, baking powder, and salt.
5. Add the dry ingredients to the wet ingredients a little bit at a time, alternating with the buttermilk.
6. Fold in the blueberries.
7. Grease a 9x9-inch baking dish and spread the batter into the pan. Sprinkle the batter with 1 tbsp of sugar.

8. Bake for 35-45 minutes or until a toothpick inserted comes out clean.
9. Let cool slightly then serve.

Breakfast Bombs

Servings: 8

What you need:

- 1 lb bacon
- 4 eggs
- 1/2 tsp salt
- 1/4 tsp pepper
- 16 frozen yeast dinner roll dough balls, defrosted
- 1/4 cup flour
- 1 cup shredded cheddar cheese
- 1/4 cup roasted red peppers, diced
- 1/4 cup butter, melted
- 1/2 tsp garlic powder
- 1/2 tsp dried parsley
- 1/4 tsp salt

What to do:

1. Cook the bacon until crisp then crumble into small pieces.
2. In a medium bowl, whisk together the eggs, milk, salt, and pepper.
3. Spray a small skillet with cooking spray and heat over medium heat.
4. Add the egg mixture to the skillet and scramble. Cook until they are no longer liquid but don't cook them until they are dry. Set aside.
5. Butter a 9x9-inch baking dish and set aside.

6. Sprinkle 1/4 cup flour onto a clean large workspace. On the workspace, flatten and stretch each ball of dough, one at a time, until they are three to four inches across, like a little pizza crust dough.

7. Lay out all of the flattened and stretched dough pieces. Spoon a tbsp of cheese onto each one. Top the cheese with a tbsp of eggs, a tbsp of bacon, and a tsp of diced red pepper.

8. Pull the top and bottom edges of the dough together and then bring together the left and right edges. Pinch the dough together to create a seal. Repeat with all of the dough.

9. Place the dough balls into the prepared dish.

10. Cover and refrigerate overnight or for several hours.

11. Preheat your oven to 350 degrees F.

12. Remove the baking dish from the refrigerator and uncover. Bake for 40 to 45 minutes or until tops are golden brown and the bombs are no longer doughy. Cover with foil if the tops start to get too dark.

13. While the bombs are baking, stir together the melted butter, garlic powder, parsley, and salt. When you remove the breakfast bombs from the oven, brush the butter mixture over them.

Cinnamon Roll Casserole

Servings: 6-8

What you need:

- 2 12-oz cans of cinnamon rolls, icing reserved
- 4 eggs
- ½ cup whipping cream
- 3 tbsp maple syrup
- 2 tsp vanilla
- 1 tsp cinnamon
- ¼ tsp nutmeg

What to do:

1. Spray your slow cooker with non-stick spray.
2. Unroll the cinnamon rolls from the cans and cut each roll into 4 pieces.
3. Place a layer of the cinnamon roll pieces in the bottom of your slow cooker.
4. In a medium bowl, whisk together the eggs, cream, maple syrup, vanilla, cinnamon, and nutmeg.
5. Pour this mixture evenly over the layer of cinnamon roll pieces in the bottom of your slow cooker.
6. Place the remaining cinnamon roll pieces in the slow cooker and spoon one container of the icing over the rolls.
7. Cover and cook on low for 2-3 hours or until the rolls are set.
8. Drizzle the remaining container of icing over the rolls.
9. Serve warm.

Eggnog French Toast

Servings: 12

What you need:

- 1 1/2 cups eggnog
- 5 eggs
- 1/2 tsp ground nutmeg
- 1 tsp rum extract
- 12 slices Texas toast
- Syrup of choice

What to do:

1. Preheat an electric griddle to 350 degrees F.
2. In a mixing bowl, whisk together the eggnog, eggs, nutmeg, and rum extract until completely mixed together.
3. Pour the mixture into a shallow baking dish and dip the Texas toast into it. Let it soak for a few seconds, then flip it over and let the other side soak for a few seconds.
4. Butter the griddle and transfer the soaked Texas toast onto the griddle and cook on each side until golden brown.
5. Serve warm with syrup of choice.

French Toast

Servings: 4-6

What you need:

- 1/2 loaf of white bread
- 6 eggs
- 1 cup milk
- 1 tsp cinnamon
- 1 tbsp brown sugar
- 1 tsp vanilla

What to do:

1. Spray your slow cooker with non-stick cooking spray.
2. In a large mixing bowl, whisk together the eggs, milk, cinnamon, brown sugar, and vanilla.
3. Dip each slice of bread into the egg mixture and then place it in your slow cooker.
4. Pour any remaining egg mixture on top of the bread in the slow cooker.
5. Cook on low 6-8 hours.
6. Serve with fresh fruit, whipped cream, or syrup.

Gingerbread Pancakes

Servings: 6

What you need:

- 1 1/2 cups flour
- 1 tsp baking powder
- 1/2 tsp baking soda
- 1/2 tsp salt
- 1 tsp cinnamon
- 1 tsp ground ginger
- 1/4 tsp pumpkin pie spice
- 1/8 tsp cloves
- 1/8 tsp nutmeg
- 1/3 cup brown sugar
- 2 tbsp molasses
- 2 eggs
- 4 tbsp melted butter
- 3/4 cup milk

What to do:

1. Preheat an electric griddle to 350 degrees F.
2. In a large bowl, whisk together all of the dry ingredients
3. In a separate bowl, whisk together the eggs, milk, molasses, and melted butter.
4. Slowly add the wet ingredients to the dry ingredients and stir until just combined.

5. Scoop the mixture, 1/4 of a cup at a time, onto the heated griddle. Flip when the tops begin to bubble. Cook for two minutes on the other side.
6. Top with your favorite syrup.

Pecan Pie French Toast

Servings: 4

What you need:

- · 3/4 cup whole milk
- · 1 cup heavy cream
- · 8 large eggs
- · 2 tbsp vanilla extract
- · 1 loaf of French bread, cut into 8 thick slices
- · 1 stick of butter
- · 1 cup packed brown sugar
- · 1/3 cup corn syrup
- · 1/4 cup maple syrup
- · 1 cup chopped pecans

What to do:

1. In a large bowl, whisk together the milk, cream, eggs, and vanilla. Set aside.
2. Arrange the slices of bread in a large shallow baking dish. Make sure the pieces of bread are not overlapping.
3. Pour the liquid over the bread and cover and refrigerate for 6 hours or overnight.
4. When ready to bake, preheat your oven to 350 degrees F.
5. In a small saucepan over medium heat, melt the butter. Remove from heat and whisk in the brown sugar, corn syrup, maple syrup, and pecans.

6. Spread the pecan mixture evenly across the bottom of a greased 3 quart casserole dish.

7. Carefully arrange the soaked bread on top of the pecan mixture. Once again, make sure the bread isn't overlapping.

8. Bake for 35 minutes then serve.

pumpkin spice oatmeal

Servings: 4

What you need:

- 1 1/2 cups milk
- 1 1/2 cups water
- 1 cup steel cut oats
- 1/2 cup maple syrup
- 3/4 cup pumpkin puree
- 1 1/2 tbsp. pumpkin pie spice
- 1/2 cup applesauce
- 1 tsp vanilla
- 1/4 tsp salt
- 1 cup toasted pecans

What to do:

1. Spray the inside of your slow cooker with non-stick spray.
2. Combine all of the ingredients except the toasted pecans in a large bowl and mix together well.
3. Pour the mixture into your slow cooker.
4. Cover and cook on low for 4-5 hours.
5. Stir the oatmeal and leave uncovered for 30 minutes to allow it to thicken.
6. Sprinkle the toasted pecans on top before serving.

sausage breakfast casserole

Servings: 6-8

What you need:

- 1-lb of cooked ground sausage
- 12 eggs
- 1 cup milk
- 1 1/2 cups shredded cheddar cheese
- 1 tbsp ground mustard
- 1 32-oz bag shredded hash browns
- Salt and pepper, to taste

What to do:

1. In a large bowl, beat the eggs and add in the milk, salt, pepper, and ground mustard.
2. In your slow cooker, make a layer of sausage, shredded hash browns, and cheese. Repeat the layers once.
3. Pour the egg mixture over the layers.
4. Cook on low for 8 hours (while you sleep!)
5. Top with cheese before serving.

Sausage Breakfast Roll-Ups

Servings: 12

What you need:

- 1-lb of ground breakfast sausage
- 3 cans of crescent roll dough
- 2 cups of shredded cheddar cheese

What to do:

1. Preheat your oven to 350 degrees F and spray two large baking sheets.
2. Brown the sausage and drain the fat.
3. Unroll the crescent rolls and lay them out on the prepared large baking sheets.
4. Add a couple spoonfuls of cooked sausage onto the wide end of the unrolled crescent roll.
5. Add a spoonful of cheese on top of the sausage.
6. Carefully roll up the crescent rolls, tucking in the sides as you do so.
7. Bake for 12-15 minutes or until golden brown.

slow cooker Breakfast casserole

Servings: 8-10

What you need:

- 1 30-oz package of frozen hash browns
- 1/2-lb ground sausage, browned and drained
- 1-lb bacon, cooked and chopped
- 2 cups shredded cheddar cheese
- 1 onion, diced
- 1 bell pepper, diced
- 1 bell pepper, diced
- 12 eggs
- 1/2 cup milk
- Salt and pepper, to taste

What to do:

1. Spray your slow cooker with nonstick spray.
2. Layer half of the hash browns into the bottom of your slow cooker.
3. Top the hash browns with half the sausage, bacon, cheese, onions, and peppers. Repeat the layers.
4. Whisk together the eggs, milk, salt, and pepper in a mixing bowl.
5. Pour the egg mixture over the ingredients in the slow cooker.

6. Cook on low for 6-8 hours or on high for 4 hours. I usually just turn on the slow cooker before I go to bed and get up during the night to check it to make sure the edges aren't burning. My slow cooker gets super-hot so I usually put mine on "keep warm" after a few hours.

SIDES

Baked Artichoke Hearts

Servings: 6

What you need:

- 3 jars artichoke hearts, drained and rinsed
- 2/3 cup Italian bread crumbs
- 1 cup parmesan cheese, divided
- 2 tsp garlic powder, divided
- Olive oil

What to do:

1. Preheat your oven to 350 degrees F and grease an 8x8 baking dish with non-stick spray.
2. Boil the artichokes for 5 minutes then drain and pat dry.
3. In a small bowl, combine the bread crumbs, parmesan cheese, and garlic powder. Divide into two equal parts and set aside in two separate bowls.
4. Spread half of the artichoke hearts evenly in a single layer in the baking dish and top with half of the bread crumbs.
5. Arrange the other half of the artichoke hearts on top of the first layer and top with the rest of the bread crumbs.
6. Drizzle with olive oil and bake for 30-40 minutes until the top is golden brown.

Brussels Sprouts au Gratin

Servings: 8

What you need:

- 4 cups Brussels sprouts, cleaned and trimmed
- 3 tbsp butter
- 4-oz white cheddar cheese, grated
- 2 cups heavy cream
- 2 tbsp all-purpose flour
- 2 cloves garlic, minced
- Salt and pepper, to taste

What to do:

1. Preheat your oven to 400 degrees F and spray a 9x9-inch baking dish with nonstick spray.
2. Bring a pot of salted water to a boil then add the Brussels sprouts. Cook for 6-8 minutes, or until beginning to soften. Remove from heat, drain, and put them in a bowl of cold water to prevent any further cooking.
3. In a medium saucepan over medium heat, melt the butter and whisk in the flour. Stir for 1 minute. Slowly whisk in the cream and add in the garlic. Cook for 3 minutes, whisking occasionally until the sauce thickens. Remove from heat and season with salt and pepper.
4. Drain the Brussels sprouts well and cut each one in half.

5. Make a layer of Brussels sprouts in the bottom of the prepared dish and top it with half of the grated cheese. Pour the cream mixture over the Brussels sprouts and cheese. Top with the remaining cheese.

6. Bake for 12-15 minutes or until bubbly and golden on top.

Buffalo Chicken Dip

Servings: 8

What you need:

- 2 chicken breasts, cooked and shredded
- 8-oz cream cheese, softened
- 2 tbsp ranch seasoning mix
- 3/4 cup buffalo sauce
- 1 cup shredded cheddar cheese
- Fritos Scoops

What to do:

1. Cook the chicken in your slow cooker for 6 hours on low then drain out the juices. Shred the chicken and set aside.
2. Place the softened cream cheese, ranch mix, and buffalo sauce in the slow cooker and stir together.
3. Stir in the chicken breasts and cheese.
4. Cook on low for 4 hours.
5. Serve with Fritos Scoops.

Butternut Squash

Servings: 2-3

What you need:

· 1 large butternut squash

What to do:

1. Wrap the squash in aluminum foil and cook in your slow cooker on high for 4 hours or low for 6 hours.
2. Remove the squash from the aluminum foil and let it cool for 15-20 minutes.
3. Unwrap the squash and slice it in half lengthwise.
4. Scoop the seeds out with a spoon.
5. Scoop the soft squash flesh out of the skin and serve it or place it in an airtight container and refrigerate.

Cheddar creamed corn

Servings: 6-8

What you need:

- 32-oz of frozen corn
- 1 8-oz block of cream cheese, cubed
- 1 cup shredded cheddar cheese
- 1/4 cup butter
- 1/2 cup heavy cream
- 1/2 tsp salt
- 1/2 tsp pepper

What to do:

1. Place all of the ingredients in your slow cooker and stir well.
2. Cook on low for 3-4 hours or until cream cheese is melted.
3. Stir well and serve.

corn casserole

Servings: 6-8

What you need:

- 8-oz cream cheese, softened
- 2 eggs, beaten
- 1/2 cup sugar
- 8 1/2-oz corn muffin mix
- 2 1/2 cups frozen corn
- 16 oz canned cream corn
- 1 cup milk
- 2 tbsp butter
- 1 tsp Cajun seasoning
- Salt and pepper, to taste

What to do:

1. In a mixing bowl, combine the cream cheese, egg, and sugar.
2. Mix in the muffin mix, corn, milk, butter, and seasonings.
3. Pour the mixture into the slow cooker and cook for 2-4 hours on high.
4. Season with salt and pepper if needed before serving.

corn Pudding

Servings: 6

What you need:

- 8 ears of fresh corn, cut off the cob
- 2 eggs
- 1 cup half and half
- Salt and pepper, to taste
- 1/4 tsp ground nutmeg
- 3/4 cup crushed saltine or oyster crackers
- 3 tbsp butter, melted
- 1/2 cup shredded cheddar cheese

What to do:

1. Preheat your oven to 350 degrees F and spray a 9x9-inch dish with non-stick cooking spray.
2. In a mixing bowl, whisk together the eggs, half and half, salt, pepper, and nutmeg.
3. Stir in the corn, half of the cracker crumbs, and 1 tbsp of melted butter.
4. Pour the mixture into the prepared pan and sprinkle the cheese over it.
5. Mix the remaining cracker crumbs with the remaining butter and sprinkle it over the cheese.
6. Bake 40-50 minutes or until golden brown and crispy on the top and edges.

cornbread Dressing

Servings: 15

What you need:

- 6 cups cornbread
- 8 slices day old bread
- 4 eggs
- 1 onion, chopped
- 1/2 cup chopped celery
- 1 1/2 tbsp poultry seasoning
- 1/2 tsp black pepper
- 2 10-oz cans cream of chicken soup
- 1 10-oz cans chicken broth
- 1/3 cup butter
- Salt and pepper, to taste

What to do:

1. Crumble the cornbread and the day old bread.
2. Spray your slow cooker with non-stick spray.
3. Add all of the ingredients except the butter, salt, and pepper to your slow cooker and stir together.
4. Dot the butter over the dressing and season with salt and pepper.
5. Cover and cook on high for 2 hours or on low for 4 hours.

cranberry feta pinwheels

Makes 36 pinwheels

What you need:

- 3/4 cup dried cranberries
- 8-oz cream cheese
- 1 cup crumbled feta cheese
- 1/4 cup chopped green onion
- 3 large flour and spinach tortillas

What to do:

1. In a large bowl, combine all of the ingredients except the tortillas.
2. Divide and spread the mixture evenly between the 3 tortillas.
3. Roll each tortilla up tightly, wrap in plastic wrap, and refrigerate for a couple hours.
4. Cut each tortilla into 12 pinwheels and serve.

cranberry orange cheese ball

Servings: 6

What you need:

- 8-oz cream cheese, at room temperature
- 1/4 cup powdered sugar
- 1 tsp fresh orange zest
- 1/2 cup dried cranberries
- 1/2 cup candied chopped pecans
- Graham crackers

What to do:

1. With an electric mixer, beat together the cream cheese and powdered sugar until smooth. Mix in the orange zest and dried cranberries until well blended.
2. Line a bowl with plastic wrap. Press the mixture into the bowl. Using the plastic wrap, roll the mixture into a ball.
3. Refrigerate the mixture for 2 hours and then roll into a ball again if it needs reshaping.
4. Unwrap and roll in the candied pecans.
5. Serve with graham crackers.

cranberry sauce

Servings: 20

What you need:

- 1 12-oz bag of cranberries
- 1/4 cup water
- 3/4 cup orange marmalade
- 3/4 cup sugar
- 1/4 tsp cinnamon

What to do:

1. Place all of the ingredients in your slow cooker and stir together.
2. Cook on high for 3 hours or until the cranberries begin to burst.
3. Once they begin to burst, gently mash the mixture with a potato masher.

Green Beans and New Potatoes

Servings: 6-8

What you need:

- 3-lbs fresh or frozen green beans
- 4-5 slices bacon, chopped
- 12 small new potatoes
- 2 cups chicken broth
- 1 small yellow onion, diced
- 1/4 cup butter
- Salt and pepper, to taste

What to do:

1. Place all of the ingredients in your slow cooker and gently combine.
2. Cook on low for 3-5 hours.

pumpkin cornbread

Servings: 10

What you need:

- 1 cup all-purpose flour
- 1 tbsp baking powder
- 1 tsp salt
- 1/2 tsp cinnamon
- 1/4 tsp ground nutmeg
- 1/2 cup light brown sugar
- 1 cup yellow cornmeal
- 2 eggs
- 1 cup pumpkin puree
- 1/4 cup olive oil
- 1 tbsp molasses

What to do:

1. Preheat your oven to 400 degrees F and spray an 8x8 baking dish with nonstick spray.
2. In a mixing bowl, whisk together the flour, baking powder, salt, spices, brown sugar, and cornmeal.
3. In another bowl, whisk together the eggs, pumpkin, oil, and molasses.
4. Stir the wet ingredients into the dry ingredients until just combined.
5. Pour into the prepared pan and bake for 25-35 minutes or until a toothpick inserted comes out clean.

Hash Brown Casserole

Servings: 10-12

What you need:

- 32-oz bag of frozen hash browns
- 8-oz sour cream
- 15-oz cream of mushroom soup
- ¼ cup finely chopped onion
- 2 cups shredded cheddar cheese
- ½ cup butter, melted
- Salt and pepper, to taste

What to do:

1. Slightly break apart the frozen hash browns.
2. Spray your slow cooker with non-stick spray.
3. In your slow cooker, mix together the hash browns, sour cream, cream of mushroom soup, onion, cheese, and melted butter.
4. Sprinkle the mixture with salt and pepper and cook for 4-5 hours on low.

Kielbasa Bites

What you need:

- 16-oz kielbasa sausage, sliced
- 3/4 cup ginger ale
- 1/2 cup brown sugar
- 1/2 cup barbecue sauce

What to do:

1. Place the sliced sausage in the bottom of a 9x9-inch baking dish.
2. In a separate bowl, whisk together the ginger ale, brown sugar, and barbecue sauce.
3. Bake at 300 degrees F for 1 1/2 hours.

* This can also be done in your slow cooker. Cook for 4-6 hours on low or 2-3 hours on high.

Loaded Baked Potato Casserole

Servings: 8

What you need:

- 4-lbs red potatoes
- 4 cloves garlic, minced
- 1/4 cup butter
- 1 cup sour cream
- 1/2 cup heavy cream
- 8-oz cream cheese
- 2 cups grated cheddar cheese
- 2 green onions, sliced
- 10 slices bacon, cooked and chopped
- Salt and pepper, to taste
- 1 green onion, sliced, for topping
- 2 slices bacon, crumbled, for topping
- 1/2 cup grated cheese, for topping

What to do:

1. Preheat your oven to 375 degrees F.
2. Wash the potatoes and peel off about 3/4 of the skin, take it all off if you want. Chop the potatoes into large chunks.
3. Boil the potatoes and garlic in a large pot of water until the potatoes are tender.

4. Drain the potatoes and mash them slightly with a potato masher.
5. Stir together all of the ingredients except for the toppings and mash together.
6. Place the potato mixture into a 9x13-inch casserole dish, sprinkle on the toppings, and bake for 25-35 minutes.

Macaroni and Cheese

Servings: 6

What you need:

- 16-oz elbow macaroni
- 1 stick of butter
- 1/2 cup of flour
- A pinch of cayenne pepper
- 1/2 tsp smoked paprika
- 1/2 tsp freshly ground black pepper
- 1 tsp salt
- 4 cups half and half
- 4 cups shredded cheddar cheese
- 3 tbsp butter, melted
- 1 cup panko bread crumbs.

What to do:

1. Spray a 9x13-inch baking dish with nonstick spray and preheat your oven to 400 degrees F.
2. In a small bowl, mix together the flour, cayenne pepper, smoked paprika, pepper, and salt.
3. In a large pot, boil the macaroni according to package directions. Drain and set aside.
4. In a large saucepan, melt the butter over medium heat.
5. Add the flour mixture into the melted butter. Whisk until smooth.

6. Add in the half and half, 1/2 cup at a time, stirring well after each addition. Stir until the mixture begins to thicken.
7. Reduce heat to low and cook for 5 minutes, stirring occasionally.
8. Remove saucepan from heat and stir in the cheddar cheese until melted.
9. Add the cooked and drained macaroni to the cheese sauce and stir well.
10. Pour the macaroni and cheese into the prepared baking dish.
11. Sprinkle the panko crumbs over the macaroni and cheese evenly.
12. Drizzle with melted butter.
13. Bake for 20 minutes.

Melting Sweet Potatoes

Servings: 6

What you need:

- 1 1/2-lbs sweet potatoes, peeled and cut into 1-inch rounds
- 4 tbsp butter, melted
- 1/4 tsp salt
- 1/2 cup maple syrup
- 1/2 cup chopped pecans

What to do:

1. Preheat your oven to 425 degrees F.
2. Toss the sweet potatoes in the melted butter and place them in a single layer on a baking sheet. Sprinkle the potatoes with salt and bake for 15-20 minutes, flipping halfway through cooking time.
3. In a small saucepan over medium heat, bring the maple syrup to a simmer and then stir in the pecans and simmer for 2 minutes. Remove from heat.
4. Place the cooked sweet potatoes on a serving platter and pour the pecan glaze over them. Serve immediately.

parmesan potatoes

Servings: 4

What you need:

- · 1 tbsp butter
- · 2-lbs russet potatoes
- · 1/4 cup olive oil, divided
- · 1 tsp Italian seasoning
- · 4 cloves garlic, minced
- · Salt and pepper, to taste
- · 1/4 cup grated parmesan cheese, divided
- · Red pepper flakes, to taste
- · Fresh chopped parsley, garnish

What to do:

1. Preheat your oven to 400 degrees F and grease an 8x10-inch casserole dish with 1 tbsp of butter.
2. Peel and cut the potatoes into 1/2-inch pieces.
3. Place the potatoes in a large mixing bowl and toss with 2 tbsp of olive oil. Sprinkle on the Italian seasoning, garlic, salt, pepper, red pepper flakes, and half the parmesan cheese. Stir to coat the potatoes with all the seasonings.
4. Pour the potatoes into the prepared casserole dish and bake for 30 minutes.
5. Remove the potatoes from the oven and sprinkle with the remaining parmesan cheese and about 1 tbsp of olive oil.
6. Bake for 25 more minutes.

7. Place them in a serving dish and pour any remaining olive oil over them and garnish them with fresh parsley.

parmesan zucchini Rounds

Servings: 2-4

What you need:

· 2 medium zucchinis
· 1/2 cup freshly grated parmesan cheese
· Garlic salt
· Pepper

What to do:

1. Preheat your oven to 425 degrees F and line a baking sheet with foil. Lightly mist the foil with cooking spray.
2. Cut the zucchini into 1/4-inch thick slices.
3. Arrange the zucchini rounds onto the prepared pan. Sprinkle with garlic salt and pepper.
4. Spoon a small layer of parmesan cheese onto each round.
5. Bake for 15-20 minutes or until the parmesan turns golden brown.

Prosciutto Wrapped Asparagus

Servings: 4

What you need:

- 2 tbsp butter, melted
- 2 tsp minced garlic
- 16 asparagus spears, thick ends snapped off
- 8 slices of prosciutto

What to do:

1. Place the asparagus spears on a large baking sheet.
2. Stir the melted butter and garlic together in a small bowl. Brush the mixture onto the asparagus spears.
3. Turn on your oven's broiler.
4. Cut each slice of prosciutto in half lengthwise. Wrap each asparagus spear with a prosciutto half.
5. Arrange the spears on the baking sheet in a single layer and broil for 5 minutes or until prosciutto is crispy and asparagus is bright green.

sausage and Barbecue Beans

Servings: 12

What you need:

- 2 15-oz cans of black beans, drained and rinsed
- 1 15-oz cans of great northern beans, drained and rinsed
- 1 15-oz can of kidney beans, drained and rinsed
- 1 onion, diced
- 1/2 cup barbecue sauce
- 1 15-oz can tomato sauce
- 1 tbsp Worcestershire sauce
- 1 tbsp mustard
- 1 tsp chili powder
- 1 tbsp apple cider vinegar
- 1/4 cup molasses
- 1 14-oz can of beef broth
- 1/2-lb bacon, cooked and chopped
- 2-lbs Kielbasa, cut into pieces

What to do:

1. Add all of the ingredients to your slow cooker and stir to combine.
2. Cook on low for 6-8 hours or high for 3-4 hours.

Slow Cooker Cheesy Creamed Corn

Servings: 6

What you need:

- 32-oz of frozen corn
- 1 8-oz block of cream cheese, cubed
- 1 cup shredded cheddar cheese
- 1/4 cup butter
- 1/2 cup heavy cream
- 1/2 tsp salt
- 1/2 tsp pepper

What to do:

1. Place all of the ingredients in your slow cooker and stir well.
2. Cook on low for 3-4 hours or until cream cheese is melted.
3. Stir well and serve.

Slow cooker cornbread Dressing

Servings: 15

What you need:

- 6 cups cornbread
- 8 slices day old bread
- 4 eggs
- 1 onion, chopped
- 1/2 cup chopped celery
- 1 1/2 tbsp poultry seasoning
- 1/2 tsp black pepper
- 2 10-oz cans cream of chicken soup
- 1 10-oz cans chicken broth
- 1/3 cup butter
- Salt and pepper, to taste

What to do:

1. Crumble the cornbread and the day old bread.
2. Spray your slow cooker with non-stick spray.
3. Add all of the ingredients except the butter, salt, and pepper to your slow cooker and stir together.
4. Dot the butter over the dressing and season with salt and pepper.
5. Cover and cook on high for 2 hours or on low for 4 hours.

Slow Cooker Cranberry Meatballs

Servings: 16

What you need:

- 12-oz chili sauce
- 12-oz canned cranberry sauce
- 10-oz red pepper jelly
- 2 tbsp brown sugar
- 1 tbsp hot sauce, more or less to taste
- 32-oz frozen fully cooked meatballs

What to do:

1. Mix all of the ingredients except the meatballs in your slow cooker.
2. Add in the meatballs and stir to coat them well.
3. Cook on low for 6 hours or on high for 2 hours.

Slow Cooker Spinach and Artichoke Dip

Servings: 8

What you need:

- 1 10-oz bag of fresh baby spinach, roughly chopped
- 1 13.75-oz can of artichoke hearts, chopped and drained
- 8-oz cream cheese, cubed
- 1 cup sour cream
- 1 cup shredded mozzarella cheese
- 1/2 cup grated parmesan cheese
- 1/3 cup diced red onion
- 4 cloves garlic
- 1/2 tsp black pepper
- 1/4 tsp salt

What to do:

1. Place all of the ingredients in your slow cooker and stir until combined.
2. Cook on low for 4 hours or on high for 2 hours. Make sure it is heated through.
3. Transfer to a serving dish (or serve straight out of your slow cooker).
4. Serve with pita chips, bread, pretzels, etc.

squash and Apples

Servings: 6-8

What you need:

- · 1 3-lb butternut squash; peeled, seeded, and cubed
- · 4 apples, cored and chopped
- · 3/4 cup dried cranberries
- · 1 small yellow onion, diced
- · 1 tbsp cinnamon
- · 1 1/2 tsp ground nutmeg

What to do:

1. Combine the squash, apples, cranberries, onion, cinnamon, and nutmeg in your slow cooker.
2. Cook on high for 4 hours or until the squash is tender.

Stuffing

Servings: 14

What you need:

- 12 cups dry bread cubes
- 4 stalks celery, chopped
- 1/2 cup chopped fresh parsley
- 2 tsp dried sage
- 1/2 tsp dried thyme
- 1/2 tsp salt
- 1/4 tsp black pepper
- 1 3/4 cup chicken broth
- 1/3 cup butter, melted

What to do:

1. Combine all the ingredients in your slow cooker, adding the chicken broth and melted butter last. Mix well.
2. Cook on low for 4-6 hours.

Sweet Potato Casserole

Servings: 8-10

What you need:

- 2 29-oz cans sweet potatoes, drained
- 1/2 cup brown sugar
- 1 tbsp cinnamon
- 1 stick butter, sliced
- 1/2 cup heavy cream
- 1 cup crushed pecans
- 3 tbsp brown sugar

What to do:

1. Place drained sweet potatoes into slow cooker.
2. Pour in the heavy cream.
3. Sprinkle brown sugar and cinnamon on top.
4. Place butter slices on top.
5. Cook on low for 4 hours.
6. After 4 hours, mash up the sweet potatoes really well and stir everything together.
7. Sprinkle with crushed pecans and brown sugar.
8. Cover and let it cook for another 20-30 minutes before serving.

sweet potato mash

Servings: 6-8

What you need:

- 2-lbs sweet potatoes, peeled and chopped
- 1/2 cup apple juice
- 1 tbsp ground cinnamon
- 1 tbsp sugar
- 1 tbsp brown sugar
- 1 tsp ground nutmeg
- 1/2 cup apple juice
- 1 cup pecans

What to do:

1. Place all of the ingredients except the pecans and the second half cup of apple juice in your slow cooker.
2. Cook on low for 4-5 hours or until the potatoes are tender.
3. When potatoes are tender, mash everything in the slow cooker with a potato masher.
4. Pour in the second half cup of apple juice and mash more.
5. Top with pecans before serving.

Sweet Potatoes

Servings: 4

What you need:

- 4 medium sized sweet potatoes
- Butter
- Brown sugar
- Mini marshmallows

What to do:

1. Scrub, wash, and dry the sweet potatoes.
2. Poke each potato with a fork several times.
3. Wrap each potato in foil twice.
4. Place potatoes in slow cooker and cook on high for 4 hours or on low for 8 hours.
5. Top with butter, brown sugar, and mini marshmallows before serving.

Sweet Potatoes with Pecans and Apples

Servings: 8

What you need:

- 3-lbs sweet potatoes
- 1 cup pecan halves
- 2 tbsp butter
- 2 tbsp refined coconut oil
- 2/3 cup honey
- 3/4 tsp ground cinnamon
- 1/2 tsp ground nutmeg
- 1/4 tsp cayenne pepper
- 1/2 tsp salt
- 1/4 cup whiskey
- 2 Granny Smith apples; cored, peeled, and chopped

What to do:

1. Bake the sweet potatoes on a baking sheet in the oven for 1 hour at 375 degrees F. Set aside until cool enough to handle, then remove the skins and cut into 3/4-inch chunks.
2. In a medium skillet over medium heat, lightly toast the pecans for about 4 minutes or until fragrant. Add the butter and coconut oil and let them melt. Next, add the honey, cinnamon, nutmeg, cayenne, and salt. Let simmer for 4-5 minutes. Slowly and carefully pour the whiskey into the skillet

and reduce heat. Stir while simmering for 5 minutes until reduced.

3. Grease a 9x9-inch baking dish and place the apples and sweet potatoes in it.

4. Pour the pecan glaze over the potatoes and apples. Bake at 375 for 20-30 minutes or until the apples are soft.

vegetable stew

Servings: 6-8

What you need:

- 2 yellow onions, diced
- 3 stalks celery, diced
- 2 large carrots, sliced
- 3 potatoes, peeled and diced
- 1 cup mushrooms, cleaned and chopped
- 1/4 cup lentils
- 3 cloves garlic, minced
- 1/2 tsp grated ginger
- 1/2 tsp thyme
- 1 bay leaf
- 2 cups water
- 1/4 cup soy sauce
- Salt and pepper, to taste
- Cornstarch

What to do:

1. Place the onions, celery, carrots, potatoes, mushrooms, lentils, garlic, ginger, thyme, bay leaf, water, and soy sauce in your slow cooker.
2. Cook for 10-12 hours on low.
3. Around 8-10 hours, add the salt, pepper, and a little bit of corn starch if you want your stew to be thicker.

MAIN DISHES

Apple Glazed Turkey Breast

Servings: 12

What you need:

- 3 1/2 lb – 5 lb turkey breast
- 1/4 cup olive oil
- 1/2 tsp salt
- 1/2 tsp pepper
- 1 tsp garlic powder
- 1/2 tsp dried parsley
- 1 large onion, chopped
- 1 apple, cored and sliced
- 2 cups chicken broth

What to do:

1. Wash and dry the turkey breast.
2. Brush the breast with olive oil and sprinkle on the salt, pepper, garlic powder, and parsley.
3. Place the chopped onion and apple into the turkey's cavity.
4. Place the turkey breast into your greased slow cooker, breast side up.
5. Pour the chicken broth over the turkey.
6. Insert a meat thermometer into the thickest part of the turkey breast.

7. Cook for 3-4 hours or until the thermometer reaches 140 degrees F.
8. Cook for another 2-3 hours on low until the thermometer reaches 170 degrees F.
9. Remove the turkey from the slow cooker and place it on a roasting pan.
10. Broil the turkey for 5-7 minutes or until the skin has browned.
11. Remove from the oven and let the turkey rest for 15 minutes.
12. Remove the onion and apple from the turkey.
13. Slice the turkey and serve.

Baked Potato Soup

Servings: 8-10

What you need:

- 5 lbs russet potatoes, washed and diced
- 1 yellow onion, diced
- 5 cloves garlic, minced
- 2 quarts chicken broth
- 2 8-oz blocks cream cheese
- 1 tsp salt
- 1 tsp bacon
- Crumbled bacon
- Shredded cheese
- Chopped green onion

What to do:

1. Add the potatoes, onion, garlic, chicken broth, and salt to a slow cooker.
2. Cook on high for 6-7 hours.
3. Cube and soften the cream cheese and add it to the slow cooker.
4. Use a potato masher to mash up the potatoes and cream cheese.
5. Stir well and cook on low for another 2 hours.
6. Top with bacon, cheese, and green onion before serving.

Chicken and Dumplings

Servings: 6-8

What you need:

- 4 skinless chicken thighs
- 4 skinless chicken drumsticks
- 1 quart chicken broth
- 3 cups water
- 1 small yellow onion, diced
- 1 stalk celery, chopped
- 1 tsp dried thyme
- 1/4 tsp salt
- 1 12-oz package frozen dumplings
- 2 tsp butter
- 1 tsp freshly ground black pepper

What to do:

1. Boil the chicken thighs and drumsticks in chicken broth and water for 45 minutes.
2. Remove the chicken from the liquid and let it cool slightly.
3. Shred the chicken off of the bones.
4. Pour the liquid into the slow cooker and set to high.
5. Separate the dumpling strips and break each strip in half.
6. Add the dumplings to the slow cooker one at a time.
7. Add the chicken, onion, celery, thyme, salt, butter, and pepper to the slow cooker.

8. Let the chicken and dumplings cook on high for 2 hours, stirring occasionally.

9. Reduce heat to low and let cook for another 2-4 hours on low.

Chicken Gnocchi Soup

Servings: 8

What you need:

- 1 tbsp extra virgin olive oil
- 1/4 cup butter
- 1/4 cup flour
- 1 stalk celery, diced
- 2 cloves garlic, minced
- 4 cups half and half
- 1 12-oz package of gnocchi
- 1 cup shredded carrots
- 1 cup cooked shredded chicken breast
- 1 quart chicken broth
- 1 cup chopped spinach
- Salt and pepper, to taste
- 1/2 tsp dried thyme
- 1/2 tsp dried parsley
- 1/4 tsp grated nutmeg

What to do:

1. Cook the gnocchi according to the package directions then drain and set it aside.
2. Heat the olive oil and butter in a large saucepan over medium heat.
3. Sauté the onion, celery, and garlic until the onion becomes translucent.

4. Whisk in the flour and constantly stir for about 1 minute then slowly stir in the half and half.
5. Add the carrots and chicken once the half and half mixture has thickened a bit.
6. Stir in the chicken broth and cook for 5 minutes.
7. Stir in the gnocchi, spinach, and seasonings then simmer for 5 minutes.
8. Serve immediately.

Christmas Ham

Servings: 4-6

What you need:

- 1 precooked, spiral cut ham
- 2 cups brown sugar
- 1 can pineapple rings

What to do:

1. Sprinkle 1 and 1/2 cups of the brown sugar into the bottom of a slow cooker.
2. Place the ham on top of the brown sugar and pour the pineapple rings and juice on top.
3. Sprinkle the rest of the brown sugar on top of the ham.
4. Cook for 6-8 hours on low.

corn chowder

Servings: 4-6

What you need:

- 16-oz canned whole kernel corn, drained
- 2 potatoes, peeled and chopped
- 1 onion, chopped
- 1/4 cup butter
- 2 cups milk
- 2 cups chicken broth
- Salt and pepper, to taste
- 1 tbsp chopped parsley

What to do:

1. Combine all of the ingredients except 1/2 cup of corn, butter, and milk in your slow cooker.
2. Cook on low for 7-9 hours, then puree in a blender, food processor, or with an immersion blender and return to the slow cooker.
3. Stir in the extra half cup of corn, butter, and milk.
4. Cook on low for another hour before serving.

cRanberRY Balsamic
Roasted Chicken

Servings: 6

What you need:

- 2.5-lbs chicken thighs, legs, and breasts, with skin
- 3 sprigs fresh thyme
- 1 tsp dried Italian seasoning
- 1/2 cup fresh cranberries
- 1 tbsp maple syrup
- 1 tbsp balsamic vinegar

-Marinade:

- 1/3 cup cranberries
- 2 tbsp olive oil
- 2 tbsp soy sauce
- 1/4 cup balsamic vinegar
- 1/4 tsp salt
- 1/4 tsp black pepper
- 2 cloves garlic, minced

What to do:

1. Place the chicken in a roasting pan and set aside.
2. Place all of the marinade ingredients in your food processor and blend until smooth.

3. Pour the marinade over the chicken. Make sure all of the chicken is coated. Place the chicken skin side down in the pan.

4. Cover and refrigerate for 30 minutes – 24 hours.

5. When ready to cook, preheat your oven to 375 degrees F.

6. Add the 1/2 cup of fresh cranberries, thyme, and Italian seasoning to the chicken.

7. Bake for 25 minutes then remove from the oven and turn all the pieces skin side up.

8. While the chicken is baking, stir together the maple syrup and 1 tbsp of balsamic vinegar. Brush this mixture onto the chicken skin.

9. Broil the chicken for 5 minutes or until the skin is crisp.

10. Before serving, spoon sauce from the bottom of the pan onto the chicken.

cranberry Glazed Ham

Servings: 16

What you need:

- 2 cups fresh cranberries
- 1/4 cup water
- 1/4 cup honey
- 2 tbsp Dijon mustard
- 1/4 cup apple cider vinegar
- 1/2 cup brown sugar
- 1/2 tsp cayenne pepper
- 6-lb cooked and sliced spiral ham

What to do:

1. Stir together the cranberries, water, and honey in a saucepan over medium heat. Stir for 5 minutes until the cranberries have popped. Stir in the Dijon mustard, vinegar, brown sugar, and cayenne pepper. Cook for another 5 minutes until the sauce has thickened then remove from heat.
2. Puree the sauce with an immersion blender or transfer the sauce to a regular blender with top vented open and covered with a hand towel or food processor.
3. Preheat your oven to 325 degrees F. Place a rack in your roasting pan.
4. Place the ham on the rack and use a brush to coat the ham with cranberry glaze.

5. Place the pan in the oven and roast for 90 minutes or until the ham is hot all the way through.
6. At the end of 90 minutes, brush more sauce on the ham and roast for another 20 minutes.
7. Serve the ham with the remaining glaze.

crustless chicken pot pie

Servings: 4-6

What you need:

- 1 can cream of chicken soup
- 1 can cream of mushroom soup
- 2 14-oz bags of frozen mixed vegetables
- 1 tsp oregano
- 1 tsp dried basil
- 1 tsp garlic powder
- 2 cups heavy cream
- 1 1/2-lbs boneless skinless chicken breasts, chopped
- Salt and pepper, to taste
- 3 cups rice

What to do:

1. Place all of the ingredients in a slow cooker and stir well.
2. Cook on high for 5-6 hours or on low for 8 hours.

Easy Christmas Ham

Servings: 10

What you need:

- 7-8-lb spiral cut ham
- 1 cup brown sugar
- 1/2 cup maple syrup
- 2 cups pineapple

What to do:

1. Place the ham inside your slow cooker, flat side down.
2. Rub the brown sugar all over the ham.
3. Pour the maple syrup and pineapple over the ham.
4. Cover and cook on low for 4-6 hours, basting the liquid over the ham every hour or so.
5. Remove the ham from the slow cooker and let it sit for 15 minutes before cutting and serving.

Garlic Prime Rib Roast

Servings: 8

What you need:

- 2 tbsp minced garlic
- 2 tbsp olive oil
- 2 tsp salt
- 1 tsp pepper
- 2-3 sprigs fresh thyme
- 5-lb boneless prime rib roast

What to do:

1. Mix together all of the ingredients but the roast.
2. Marinate the roast in the mixture overnight. I put my roast in a large roasting pan and poured the mixture over it, covered it with the lid, and refrigerated it overnight.
3. Two hours before you get ready to cook the roast, remove it from the refrigerator and let it come to room temperature.
4. Preheat your oven to 450 degrees F and roast uncovered for 15 minutes. Reduce the heat to 300 degrees F and roast for 2 hours or until a thermometer reads 130-135 degrees F. It will be medium rare. For rare, cook to an internal temperature of 120-125 degrees F. For well done, cook to an internal temperature of 145 degrees F.

Jambalaya

Servings: 6-8

What you need:

- 1-lb boneless skinless chicken breasts
- 1/2-lb Andouille sausage, diced
- 1 28-oz can diced tomatoes
- 1 can rotel tomatoes
- 1 yellow onion, chopped
- 1 green bell pepper, chopped
- 1 stalk celery, chopped
- 2 cups chicken broth
- 2 tsp dried oregano
- 2 tsp Cajun seasoning
- 2 bay leaves
- 2 cups white long grain rice
- Fresh parsley

What to do:

1. In the slow cooker, combine all of the ingredients except the rice and parsley.
2. Cook on low for high for 4 hours.
3. Remove chicken, shred it, and return it to the slow cooker.
4. Add rice to the slow cooker and stir.
5. Cook on low for 2-4 hours or until rice is cooked. Stir occasionally.
6. Discard the bay leaves and top with parsley before serving.

Lasagna

Servings: 8

What you need:

- 2 to 3-lbs. ground beef, cooked and drained
- 1 large can of prepared spaghetti sauce
- 1/2 tsp garlic powder
- 1 tsp minced onions
- Salt & pepper to taste
- 1 container Ricotta cheese
- 1/2 block of cream cheese
- 1 1/2 cups mozzarella cheese
- 3/4 cup cheddar cheese
- 1/2 cup parmesan cheese
- 3 eggs
- 1 1/2 tbsp parsley
- 1/4 cup water
- Oven ready lasagna noodles

What to do:

1. Mix together the cooked ground beef, spaghetti sauce, garlic powder, onions, salt and pepper. Stir and cook over medium high heat until heated through (about 5 minutes).
2. In a separate bowl, mix together the Ricotta cheese, cream cheese, the parmesan cheese, 1/2 cup of the mozzarella cheese, and 1/4 cup of the cheddar cheese, eggs and parsley.

3. In your lasagna pan spread a layer of the meat sauce, then a layer of lasagna noodles (uncooked), then a layer of the cheese mixture, topped with 1/2 cup of mozzarella cheese and 1/4 cup of cheddar cheese. Repeat layers.
4. Cover with foil and bake at 300 degrees F for an hour and a half.

Rosemary and Garlic Roast

Servings: 8-10

What you need:

- 3-lb boneless rib eye roast
- 1/4 cup chopped fresh rosemary
- 1/4 cup minced garlic
- Salt and pepper, to taste
- 4 tbsp olive oil, divided
- 4 tbsp butter, divided
- 4 cups of mushrooms, sliced small
- 1 cup of beef stock

What to do:

1. Preheat your oven to 350 degrees F.
2. Sprinkle the roast with salt and pepper.
3. In a small bowl, mix together 2 tbsp of olive oil, the rosemary, and the garlic. Set aside.
4. In a cast iron skillet over medium heat, add 2 tbsp of olive oil and once hot, sear the roast on all sides.
5. Brush the rosemary mixture onto the roast.
6. Place the roast (in the cast iron skillet) in your preheated oven and cook for 1 – 1 1/2 hours until a meat thermometer reads 135-140 degrees F.
7. Remove it from the oven and let it rest for 10-15 minutes.

8. While the roast is resting, sauté the mushrooms in 2 tbsp of butter for 5-8 minutes.

9. Remove the roast from the cast iron skillet. Place the skillet onto the stovetop and turn the stove on medium. Pour the beef stock into the pan and deglaze the pan, scraping the bits from the bottom. Allow it to simmer until thick. Add the sautéed mushrooms to this sauce and stir in the remaining 2 tbsp of butter.

10. Place the roast back into the cast iron skillet with the sauce then serve.

Slow Cooker Brown Sugar Maple Ham

Servings: 10

What you need:

- 7-8-lb spiral cut ham
- 1 cup brown sugar
- 1/2 cup maple syrup
- 2 cups pineapple rings

What to do:

1. Place the ham inside your slow cooker, flat side down.
2. Rub the brown sugar all over the ham.
3. Pour the maple syrup and pineapple over the ham.
4. Cover and cook on low for 4-6 hours, basting the liquid over the ham every hour or so.
5. Remove the ham from the slow cooker and let it sit for 15 minutes before slicing and serving.

Slow Cooker Chicken and Stuffing

Servings: 4

What you need:

- 4 boneless skinless chicken breasts
- 1 tsp dried parsley
- 1 10.5-oz can of cream of chicken soup
- 8-oz sour cream
- 1 6-oz box of stuffing mix
- 3/4 cup chicken broth

What to do:

1. Sprinkle the chicken with parsley and place it in the bottom of your slow cooker.
2. In a large bowl, mix together the cream of chicken, sour cream, stuffing, and half of the broth and pour it over the chicken.
3. Lay the stuffing evenly on top of the mixture in the slow cooker.
4. Cook on high for 4 hours or on low for 8 hours. Check it every now and then and add more broth if needed and stir.

Slow Cooker Ham

Servings: 12

What you need:

· 5-lb bone in ham
· 1 cup apple cider vinegar
· 1 cup brown sugar
· 3 tbsp dry mustard

What to do:

1. Place the ham in your slow cooker.
2. In a small bowl, mix together the dry mustard and brown sugar. Press it onto the ham.
3. Pour the apple cider vinegar into the bottom of the slow cooker.
4. Cook on low for 8 hours, flipping over 1/2 way through cooking time.

Slow Cooker Red Wine Ribs

Servings: 4

What you need:

- 8 beef short ribs
- Salt and pepper, to taste
- 1 tbsp olive oil
- 5 cloves of garlic
- 1/4 cup tomato paste
- 16-oz dry red wine
- 1 tbsp beef base or 1 beef bouillon cube
- 3 cups hot water

What to do:

1. Season the ribs generously with salt and pepper.
2. Heat the olive oil in a skillet and brown the ribs for 4 minutes on each side.
3. Transfer the ribs to your slow cooker.
4. Pour the tomato paste and garlic cloves into the same skillet and cook until the garlic begins to soften.
5. Pour in the wine and bring to a simmer and cook until the wine reduces by half, about 15 minutes.
6. Pour the liquid into the slow cooker and add the beef base and hot water.
7. Cover and cook on low for 6 hours or until meat is tender.

Slow cooker sausage stuffing

Servings: 10

What you need:

- 1 loaf of French bread, diced into cubes and dried for 24 hours
- 1 stick of butter, diced into pieces
- 1 large onion, diced
- 1 cup celery, diced
- 3 tbsp fresh rosemary, chopped
- 1 tbsp fresh sage, chopped
- 2 tbsp fresh thyme, chopped
- 1 tsp salt
- 1 tsp black pepper
- 1 1/2 cups chicken broth
- 1-lb ground Italian sausage
- 1/4 cup Italian parsley, chopped

What to do:

1. Place the dried bread cubes into your slow cooker.
2. On top of the bread, place the diced butter, diced onion, diced celery, chopped herbs, salt, pepper, and chicken broth. Stir to combine.
3. Evenly crumble the sausage in very small pieces over the bread mixture.

4. Cover and cook on low for 5 hours or until the vegetables are tender and the sausage is cooked through.
5. Add the parsley and stir and cook for 5 more minutes then serve.

DESSERTS

Bread Pudding

Servings: 4-6

What you need:

· 10 slices raisin cinnamon swirl bread, cut into cubes
· 1 14-oz can sweetened condensed milk
· 1 cup water
· 1 tsp vanilla
· 5 eggs, beaten

What to do:

1. Place the bread cubes into your slow cooker.
2. Mix the sweetened condensed milk, water, vanilla, and eggs together in a bowl and pour the mixture over the bread.
3. Stir to coat the bread evenly.
4. Cook on low for 3-4 hours or until set.

Apple Crisp

Servings: 4

What you need:

- 5 large apples; peeled, cored, and sliced
- 1 tsp nutmeg
- 1 tsp cinnamon
- 1 tbsp maple syrup
- 1 tbsp lemon juice
- 1 cup oats
- 1/2 cup brown sugar
- 1/2 cup all-purpose flour
- 4 tbsp butter
- 1/4 tsp salt

What to do:

1. Add the sliced apples, half the nutmeg, half the cinnamon, maple syrup, and lemon juice to your slow cooker and mix together well.
2. In a mixing bowl, mix together the oats, butter, sugar, flour, the other half the nutmeg, the other half of cinnamon. Spread this mixture over the apples in the slow cooker.
3. Cook on low for 4 hours before serving.

Butterfinger Cookies

Makes 2 1/2 dozen

What you need:

- 1 3/4 cups all-purpose flour
- 3/4 tsp baking soda
- 1/4 tsp salt
- 3/4 cup granulated sugar
- 1/2 cup butter, softened
- 1 large egg
- 8 fun sized Butterfingers, chopped

What to do:

1. Preheat your oven to 350 degrees F.
2. In a mixing bowl, combine the flour, baking soda, and salt. Set aside.
3. In a separate mixing bowl, beat the sugar and butter with an electric mixer until creamy then mix in the egg.
4. Slowly mix in the flour mixture.
5. Stir in the Butterfinger pieces with a spoon.
6. Drop tablespoonfuls of dough onto prepared baking sheet 2 inches apart.
7. Bake for 10-12 minutes or until lightly golden.
8. Allow the cookies to cool for 5 minutes then transfer them to a wire rack to cool completely.

cake Batter christmas cookies

Makes 2 dozen

What you need:

- 1 1/4 cups all-purpose flour
- 1 1/4 cup yellow boxed cake mix
- 1/2 tsp baking soda
- 3/4 cup butter, softened
- 1/2 cup sugar
- 1/2 cup brown sugar
- 1 egg
- 1 1/2 tsp vanilla extract
- 1 cup white chocolate chips
- 1/2 cup Christmas colored sprinkles

What to do:

1. In a large bowl, sift together the flour, cake mix, and baking soda.
2. In another large bowl, mix together (with a hand mixer) the butter and both sugars until smooth.
3. Add in the egg and mix for 1 minute until combined. Scrape down the sides of the bowl as needed.
4. Add the vanilla and mix until combined.
5. Add the flour mixture a little bit at a time at low speed until all of it is mixed in well.

6. Mix in the chocolate chips and sprinkles on low speed.
7. Cover and refrigerate the dough for at least 2 hours.
8. Preheat your oven to 350 degrees F and line 2 large baking sheets with parchment paper.
9. Form the dough into balls about 1 and a half tbsp each. Make the balls taller than they are round to make thicker cookies.
10. Bake the cookies for 10-12 minutes or until the edges are browned.
11. Allow the cookies to cool for 5 minutes on the baking sheet for 5 minutes then transfer them to a wire rack to cool completely.

candied pecans

Servings: 16

What you need:

- 1 cup sugar
- 3/4 cup brown sugar
- 1 1/2 tbsp cinnamon
- 1 egg white
- 2 tsp vanilla
- 4 cups pecans
- 1/4 cup water

What to do:

1. In a large bowl, mix together the sugar, brown sugar, and cinnamon.
2. In a separate bowl, whisk together the egg white and vanilla until it is a little bit frothy.
3. Spray your slow cooker with cooking spray.
4. Put the pecans in the slow cooker.
5. Pour the egg mixture over the pecans and stir well.
6. Sprinkle the cinnamon sugar mixture over the pecans and stir well.
7. Cover and cook on low for 3 hours, stirring every 30 minutes.
8. When there are 30 minutes left, pour 1/4 cup water into the slow cooker and stuff.
9. Spread the pecans on a baking pan and let them cool for 15-20 minutes.

candY cane FUdge

Makes 36 squares

What you need:

- 3 cups white chocolate chips
- 1 14-oz can sweetened condensed milk
- 1 tsp vanilla extract
- 8 crushed candy canes

What to do:

1. Line a 9x9-inch baking dish with parchment paper and grease it.
2. In a large saucepan, combine the white chocolate chips and sweetened condensed milk. Continue stirring until all of the white chocolate chips have completely melted.
3. Stir in the vanilla extract and the crushed candy canes.
4. Transfer to the prepared baking dish and allow it to cool for about an hour.
5. Place the baking dish in the refrigerator and allow it to set for an additional 3-4 hours.

candy caramels

Makes 48 pieces

What you need:

- 6-oz chocolate flavor candy coating, chopped
- 6-oz vanilla flavor candy coating, chopped
- 1 cup toffee pieces, crushed
- Christmas colored sprinkles.
- 48 decorative toothpicks
- 14-oz package of caramels, unwrapped
- 2-oz chocolate candy coating, chopped

What to do:

1. In a microwave safe glass bowl, place the 6-oz chocolate and 6-oz vanilla and microwave for 3 minutes, stirring every 30 seconds.
2. Place the toffee pieces and Christmas colored sprinkles in a shallow dish.
3. Insert a toothpick into each caramel piece.
4. Dip each caramel piece into the melted chocolate and vanilla mixture.
5. Coat each dipped caramel into the toffee and sprinkle mixture.
6. Place the coated pieces onto a sheet of wax paper and let cool before serving.

candy cane Marshmallow Pops

Makes 36

What you need:

- 1 bag large marshmallows
- 1 large bag mini candy canes
- 1 large block of chocolate
- Crushed candy canes

What to do:

1. You can adjust this recipe to make whatever amount of servings you want!
2. Stick a mini candy cane into each large marshmallow.
3. Melt the chocolate in the microwave or over a double boiler.
4. Dip each marshmallow into the chocolate.
5. Roll each chocolate dipped marshmallow in the crushed candy canes.
6. Place on wax paper to dry.

caramel Marshmallow popcorn

Servings: 16

What you need:

- 1 bag popped popcorn
- 1/2 cup butter
- 1 cup brown sugar
- 1 tbsp corn syrup
- 20 large marshmallows

What to do:

1. Pour the popped popcorn into a large bowl and remove any unpopped kernels.
2. Melt the butter in a large pot over medium heat.
3. Add the brown sugar and corn syrup into the melted butter.
4. Add the marshmallows and stir constantly on low heat until melted.
5. Pour the mixture over the popcorn and stir well.
6. Spread onto parchment paper and let cool.
7. Cut into squares before serving.

carrot cake

Servings: 8-10

What you need:

- 1 cup sugar
- 2 eggs
- 1/4 cup water
- 1/3 cup vegetable oil
- 1 1/2 cups flour
- 1 tsp vanilla
- 1 tsp baking powder
- 1/2 tsp baking soda
- 1 tsp cinnamon
- 1 cup packed grated carrots
- Cream cheese frosting

What to do:

1. In a mixing bowl, cream the sugar, eggs, water and oil. Add the flour, vanilla, baking powder, baking soda, and cinnamon. Blend until combined. Stir in the carrots by hand.
2. Spray the inside of your slow cooker with non-stick cooking spray.
3. Pour the batter into your slow cooker and spread it evenly.
4. Cook for 2-3 hours on low or until a toothpick inserted into the middle comes out clean.
5. Remove the cake from the slow cooker, let it cool, and top it with cream cheese frosting.

Cherry Cordials

Makes: 30

What you need:

- 10-oz Maraschino cherries
- 1 tbsp butter, softened
- 1 tsp corn syrup
- Warm water*
- 1 tbsp juice from maraschino cherry jar
- 1 1/2 cups powdered sugar
- 12-oz semi-sweet chocolate chips

What to do:

1. Line a baking sheet with paper towels and remove the cherries from the jar and place them on the baking sheet. Remove the stems if they have them.
2. Line another baking sheet with parchment paper.
3. In a mixing bowl, add the powdered sugar. Add 1 tbsp of warm water to it until it is dissolved. Add as little water as possible.
4. When the powdered sugar is just barely dissolved, add the softened butter, corn syrup, and 1 tbsp juice from cherry jar.**
5. Form this mixture into 1/2-inch balls and flatten them.
6. Place a cherry in the middle of each flattened ball and wrap the cherry up. Place each ball on the prepared baking sheet.
7. Place the baking sheet in the freezer for 30 minutes to 1 hour.

8. Melt the chocolate in a microwave safe bowl for about 3 minutes or until melted and smooth, stirring every 30 seconds.
9. Dip the balls in the chocolate using a fork or toothpick. Shake off the excess chocolate and return each ball to the baking sheet.
10. Refrigerate for at least 30 minutes on the baking sheet.
11. Serve or store in an airtight container.

*The original recipe calls for 1/2 tsp Invertase, which is an enzyme used in candy making and it helps to dissolve sugar. I couldn't find it at good old trusty Walmart so I just used water.

**If you happen to have or can find some Invertase, mix it in with the butter, corn syrup, and cherry juice; then add the powdered sugar.

Chocolate caramel cookies

Makes 2 1/2 dozen

What you need:

- 1 package devil's food cake mix
- 2 eggs
- 1/2 cup canola oil
- 42 Rolo candies
- Christmas colored M&M's

What to do:

1. Preheat your oven to 350 degrees F and line 2 baking sheets with parchment paper.
2. In a large bowl, mix together the cake mix, eggs, and oil.
3. Roll the dough into tbsp sized balls and place 1-2 inches apart on the prepared baking sheets.
4. Press a Rolo into each ball.
5. Bake for 8-10 minutes.
6. As soon as you remove the cookies from the oven, press 4 M&M's onto each cookie.
7. Let cool and serve!

Chocolate Peppermint Cookies

Servings: 15

What you need:

- 3/4 cup butter, softened
- 1/2 cup brown sugar, packed
- 1/2 cup sugar
- 1 egg
- 1/2 tsp vanilla extract
- 1/2 tsp peppermint extract
- 1 1/4 cups all-purpose flour
- 1/2 cup cocoa
- 1 tsp baking soda
- 1/2 cup Andes Peppermint Crunch pieces
- 3/4 cup chopped Oreos

What to do:

1. In a mixing bowl, cream together the butter and sugar until light and fluffy.
2. Mix in the egg and vanilla extract.
3. In a separate bowl, whisk together the flour, cocoa, and baking powder until combined.
4. Gradually add the flour mixture to the butter and sugar mixture and mix until combined well.
5. Cover and refrigerate for at least an hour.

6. Preheat your oven to 350 degrees F and line a baking sheet with parchment paper.
7. Form the dough into 1 to 2-inch balls and place them on the baking sheet 1 inch apart.
8. Bake for 8-10 minutes or until the edges look firm. The middle should still look soft.
9. Remove from the oven and cool for 2 minutes before transferring to a wire rack to cool completely.

Chocolate Peppermint Patties

Makes 8 dozen

What you need:

- 1-lb powdered sugar
- 4-oz cream cheese, softened
- 1/2 tsp peppermint extract
- 6-oz chocolate chips

What to do:

1. In a large mixing bowl, whip the cream cheese with an electric mixer.
2. Gradually add the powdered sugar and mix on low until it is all incorporated.
3. Add in the peppermint extract and mix well.
4. Roll the dough into teaspoon sized balls and place on a baking sheet lined with wax paper or parchment paper.
5. Make a small well in the center of each ball.
6. Cover the baking pan(s) and refrigerate for at least 2 hours.
7. Melt the chocolate chips in the microwave at 30 second intervals until melted and smooth, stirring between every interval.
8. Fill a piping bag or a freezer bag with a tiny piece of one corner cut off with the melted chocolate.

9. Fill each peppermint well with chocolate and let cool before serving.

Christmas Cookie Bark

Servings: 16-18

What you need:

- · 14 Christmas Oreos, broken into pieces
- · 1 1/2 cups pretzels, broken into pieces
- · 1 cup Christmas colored M&M's
- · 1-lb white chocolate or almond bark
- · Christmas colored sprinkles

What to do:

1. Line a baking sheet with parchment paper.
2. Mix together the Oreo pieces, pretzels, and 3/4 cup of the M&M's.
3. Melt the white chocolate or bark in a microwave safe bowl for 2-3 minutes, stirring every 30 seconds until completely melted.
4. Drizzle the melted chocolate over the mixture on the baking sheet.
5. Top the chocolate with the rest of the M&M's and sprinkles.
6. Allow the bark to cool before breaking up and serving.

CHRISTMAS COOKIES

Makes 2 dozen

What you need:

- · 1 roll of sugar cookie dough
- · 1 cup powdered sugar
- · 1/2 tsp vanilla extract
- · 2 tbsp milk
- · Christmas colored food coloring
- · 1 cup powdered sugar
- · 1/2 tsp vanilla extract
- · 2 1/2 tbsp milk
- · 2 small tipped squeeze bottles
- · Christmas cookie cutters

What to do:

1. Preheat your oven to 350 degrees F.
2. On a large sheet of wax paper, roll out the sugar cookie dough to about 1/4-inch thickness with a rolling pin.
3. Cut shapes out of the cookie dough and bake according to package directions. I used a snowflake cookie cutter.
4. Once the cookies are completely cooled, return them to the wax paper on your counter.
5. First, prepare a thicker icing for the border of the cookies. Mix together 1 cup powdered sugar, 1/2 tsp vanilla, and 2 tbsp of milk in a small bowl. You can add food coloring if you would like, I chose to keep the thicker icing white. Place a funnel in

the mouth of one of the squeeze bottles and funnel the icing into it. The icing should be thick enough to just barely pour out. You may need to add another teaspoon or 2 of milk.

6. Next, prepare the filler icing. Mix together 1 cup powdered sugar, 1/2 tsp vanilla, and 2 1/2 tbsp of milk in a small bowl. Add food coloring if you would like. I used red. You could divide the icing in half or quarters and make multiple colors (make more icing if needed). Transfer the icing into a different squeeze bottle using a clean funnel. The filler icing should be thinner, add a teaspoon or 2 of milk if it isn't thin enough for your liking.

7. Decorate the borders of your cookies with the thicker icing and let the icing dry almost completely before decorating with the filler icing.

8. Decorate with the filler icing and let the icing dry completely before serving the cookies.

christmas crack

Servings: 10-12

What you need:

- Saltine crackers
- 1 stick of butter
- 1 cup brown sugar
- 1 tsp vanilla extract
- 1 bag of milk chocolate chips

What to do:

1. Preheat your oven to 400 degrees F.
2. Line a baking sheet with aluminum foil and spray with cooking spray.
3. Cover the cookie sheet with one layer of saltine crackers.
4. In a saucepan over medium heat, bring the butter and brown sugar to a boil while constantly stirring for 3 minutes.
5. Remove the saucepan from the heat and add in the vanilla extract.
6. Pour the mixture over the crackers and bake for 5-6 minutes.
7. Remove the baking pan from the oven and immediately pour the bag of chocolate chips over the top.
8. Allow the chocolate chips to melt for a minute or two and then spread it out evenly.
9. Allow it to cool then break into pieces.

cinnamon pecans

Servings: 4-6

What you need:

- 1 1/4 cup sugar
- 1 1/4 cup brown sugar
- 2 tbsp cinnamon
- 1/8 tsp salt
- 1 egg white
- 2 tsp vanilla
- 3 cups pecans
- 1/4 cup water

What to do:

1. In a large bowl, mix together the sugar, brown sugar, cinnamon, and salt.
2. In a separate bowl, mix together the egg white and vanilla.
3. Add the pecans to the egg mixture and coat them thoroughly.
4. Add the cinnamon mixture to the pecans and stir until they are evenly coated.
5. Pour the pecan mixture into your crockpot and cook on low for 3-4 hours, stirring occasionally.

Cinnamon Sugar Pecans

Servings: 12

What you need:

- 1-lb pecan halves
- 1 large egg white
- 1 tbsp water
- 1/2 tsp vanilla extract
- 1 cup sugar
- 1/2 tsp salt

What to do:

1. Preheat your oven to 250 degrees F.
2. Line a baking sheet with parchment paper.
3. In a large mixing bowl, whisk together the egg white and vanilla until frothy.
4. In another mixing bowl, whisk together the sugar, cinnamon, and salt.
5. Add the pecans to the egg white mixture and coat evenly.
6. Pour half of the sugar mixture over the coated pecans, stir well, and then add the other half of the sugar mixture.
7. Pour the coated pecans onto the prepared baking sheet in an even layer.
8. Bake for 1 hour, stirring every 20 minutes.
9. Allow the pecans to cool then store in an airtight container.

Slow Cooker Christmas Crack

Servings: 10-12

What you need:

- 8-oz unsalted peanuts
- 8-oz salted peanuts
- 6-oz semi-sweet chocolate chips
- 6-oz milk chocolate chips
- 10-oz peanut butter chips
- 1-lb white almond bark

What to do:

1. Layer all ingredients in your slow cooker, with the peanuts on the bottom.
2. Cover and cook on low for 2 hours.
3. Stir well and let cook for another 30 minutes to 1 hour.
4. Stir again then spoon the mixture onto wax paper or parchment paper.
5. Let cool for at least 1 hour.

Divinity

Servings: 24

What you need:

- 2 2/3 cups sugar
- 2/3 cup light corn syrup
- 2/3 cup water
- 2 egg whites
- 1 tsp vanilla

What to do:

1. In a heavy saucepan over medium heat, stir together the sugar, syrup, and water. Bring to a boil, without stirring, and continue boiling until a thermometer reaches 260 degrees F.
2. Beat the two egg whites until they are stiff and easily form peaks.
3. Pour the syrup mixture into the egg white mixture and beat well.
4. Add in the vanilla and beat well.
5. When the divinity loses its shine and begins to hold its shape, spoon drops of it onto parchment paper.
6. Store in an airtight container at room temperature.

Easy Peanut Brittle

Makes 1.5 lbs

What you need:

- 1 cup sugar
- 1/2 cup corn syrup
- 1 cup peanuts
- 1 tsp butter
- 1 tsp vanilla extract
- 1 tsp baking soda

What to do:

1. Line a baking sheet with parchment paper and spray with non-stick spray.
2. In a 2 quart glass bowl, combine the sugar and corn syrup. Microwave on high for 4 minutes.
3. Stir in the peanuts and microwave for another 3 and a half minutes.
4. Stir in butter and vanilla and microwave for another minute and a half.
5. Stir in the baking soda and mix well.
6. Pour the mixture onto the prepared baking sheet and spread it out in a thin layer.
7. Let it cool completely then break into pieces before serving.

Easy Toffee

Servings: 6

What you need:

- 1 cup almonds
- 1 cup butter, cubed
- 1 cup sugar
- ½ tsp vanilla extract
- ¼ tsp salt
- 1 ½ cups semi-sweet chocolate chips
- 1/3 cup chopped pecans

What to do:

1. Preheat your oven to 350 degrees F.
2. Line a baking sheet with parchment paper.
3. Spread the almonds in an even layer on the prepared baking sheet. Toast the almonds in the oven for about 10 minutes then remove from the oven and set aside.
4. In a saucepan over medium heat, combine the butter, sugar, vanilla, and salt. Whisk constantly until the butter has melted and becomes slightly brown. This is the caramel mixture.
5. Immediately pour the caramel mixture over the toasted almonds.
6. Sprinkle the chocolate chips over the caramel.
7. Sprinkle the pecans over the chocolate chips.
8. Let cool completely and then break into pieces.

Eggnog Cookies

Makes about 32 cookies

What you need:

-Cookies:

- 2 1/4 cups all-purpose flour
- 2 tsp baking powder
- 1/2 tsp salt
- 1/2 tsp ground nutmeg
- 1/2 tsp ground cinnamon
- 3/4 cup butter, at room temperature
- 1/2 cup sugar
- 1/2 cup brown sugar
- 2 large egg yolks
- 1 tsp vanilla extract
- 1/2 tsp rum extract
- 1/2 cup eggnog

-Frosting:

- 1/2 cup butter
- 3-5 tbsp eggnog
- 1/2 tsp rum extract
- 3 cups powdered sugar

What to do:

1. Preheat your oven to 350 degrees F and line 2 baking sheets with parchment paper.
2. In a mixing bowl, whisk together the flour, baking powder, salt, nutmeg, and cinnamon. Set aside.
3. In a separate mixing bowl, cream together the butter, sugar, and brown sugar until fluffy with an electric mixer.
4. Mix in the egg yolks, one at a time, until just combined.
5. Mix in the vanilla extract, rum extract, and eggnog.
6. Slowly add the dry ingredients to the wet ingredients and mix on low until combined.
7. Scoop tablespoonfuls onto the prepared baking sheets, 2 inches apart.
8. Bake for 11-13 minutes.
9. Let cool on the baking sheets for 5 minutes before transferring to a wire rack to cool completely.
10. For frosting, whip the butter, rum extract, and 3 tbsp eggnog together. Gradually add the powdered sugar. Add additional eggnog until the frosting is desired consistency.
11. Frost the cooled cookies before serving.

Frozen peppermint pie

Servings: 16

What you need:

- · 2 premade Oreo cookie pie crusts
- · 8-oz whipped cream, thawed
- · 1.5 quart container of peppermint ice cream
- · Crushed candy canes
- · 8 Oreos, crushed

What to do:

1. Soften the ice cream until it can be easily mixed.
2. Mix the ice cream and whipped cream.
3. Spread the mixture into the two pie crusts.
4. Freeze for several hours then top with crushed candy canes and crushed Oreos.

Fudge

Servings: 8-10

What you need:

- 1 cup dark chocolate chips
- 1 cup of coconut milk
- 1/4 cup of honey

What to do:

1. Mix the ingredients directly into your slow cooker.
2. Cook on low for 2 hours.
3. Stir until the mixture is smooth.
4. Pour the fudge mixture into a greased casserole dish.
5. Cover the fudge with plastic wrap and refrigerate for at least 3 hours before serving.

Gingerbread Cookies

Makes 24 cookies

What you need:

- 1/2 cup butter, softened
- 1/2 cup butter flavored shortening
- 1 1/2 cups sugar
- 1 egg
- 1 tbsp vanilla
- 3 tbsp molasses
- 3 cups all-purpose flour
- 2 tbsp baking soda
- 2 tsp ground cinnamon
- 1 tsp ground ginger
- 1/2 tsp ground cloves
- 1/2 tsp salt
- Frosting

What to do:

1. In a large mixing bowl, cream together the butter, shortening, and sugar. Add in the egg, vanilla and molasses and mix well.
2. In a separate bowl, whisk together the flour, baking soda, cinnamon, ginger, ground cloves, and salt.
3. Add the flour mixture to the butter mixture a little bit at a time until it is all mixed in well. It will be thick!
4. Cover and refrigerate the dough for at least 2 hours.
5. Preheat your oven to 375 degrees F.

6. Lightly flour a large cutting board or sheet of wax paper.
7. Roll the dough on the floured surface and roll out into a sheet 1/4-inch thick.
8. Using a gingerbread man (or whatever shape you want!) cookie cutter, cut the dough.
9. Place the cut dough onto a greased baking sheet.
10. Bake for 10-12 minutes.
11. Let the cookies cool then decorate them with frosting.

Gingerbread Pudding

Servings: 8-10

What you need:

- 1 14-oz package of gingerbread mix
- 1/2 cup milk
- 1/2 cup raisins
- 2 1/4 cups water
- 1 cup packed brown sugar
- 3/4 cup butter

What to do:

1. Coat your slow cooker with non-stick cooking spray.
2. In a medium bowl, combine the gingerbread mix and milk. Stir in the raisins. Spread the mixture into your slow cooker.
3. In a saucepan over medium-high heat, combine the water, brown sugar, and butter. Bring to a boil, reduce heat, and simmer for 5 minutes.
4. Pour the sugar mixture over the batter in the slow cooker.
5. Cook for 2 hours.
6. Turn off the slow cooker and let it sit for 1 hour without the lid.
7. Serve with vanilla ice cream.

Gingersnaps

Makes 2 dozen

What you need:

- 3/4 cup shortening
- 1 cup granulated sugar
- 1/4 cup molasses
- 1 egg
- 2 cups all-purpose flour
- 2 tsp baking soda
- 1/4 tsp salt
- 1 tsp cinnamon
- 1 tsp ground cloves
- 1 tsp ground ginger
- 1/4 cup granulated sugar

What to do:

1. Preheat your oven to 350 degrees F and line a baking sheet with parchment paper.
2. Cream together the shortening and sugar in a mixing bowl with an electric mixer.
3. Add the molasses and egg and beat until well combined.
4. In a separate bowl, mix together the flour, baking soda, salt, cinnamon, cloves, and ginger.
5. Slowly add the dry ingredients to the wet ingredients and mix until combined.
6. Place 1/4 cup sugar into a small bowl.

7. Roll the dough into 1-inch balls and roll in the sugar.
8. Place the dough balls on the prepared pan, 2 inches apart and bake for 9-11 minutes or until set.
9. Let cool on the baking sheet for 5 minutes before transferring to a wire rack to cool completely.

Grinch Cookies

Makes about 3 dozen

What you need:

- 1 box French vanilla cake mix
- 1/2 cup vegetable oil
- 2 eggs
- 2 drops green food coloring
- Powdered sugar
- Red heart shaped candies

What to do:

1. Preheat your oven to 350 degrees F and line a baking sheet or two with parchment paper.
2. In a large mixing bowl, mix together the cake mix, food coloring, oil, and eggs with an electric mixer.
3. Chill the dough for 30 minutes.
4. Roll the dough into 1-inch balls and place on the prepared baking sheet 1-2 inches apart.
5. Dust each cookie dough ball with powdered sugar and place a heart-shaped candy in the center of each.
6. Bake for 8-9 minutes then let cool on the baking sheets for 5 minutes before transferring to a wire rack to cool completely.
7. Serve or store in an airtight container.

Hay Stacks

Makes 24

What you need:

- 1 cup butterscotch chips
- 1/2 cup peanut butter
- 1/2 cup peanuts
- 2 cups chow mein noodles

What to do:

1. Microwave the butterscotch chips and the peanut butter in a large microwave safe bowl for 2-3 minutes, stirring every 30 seconds.
2. Remove the bowl from the microwave and stir in the peanuts and the chow mein noodles.
3. Spoon dollops of the mixture onto wax paper or parchment paper. Let sit for 2-3 hours or until completely cooled and hardened.
4. Serve immediately or store in an airtight container.

Hot Chocolate Cookies

Makes 1 dozen

What you need:

- 1 roll of chocolate chip cookie dough, at room temperature
- 1 cup Nutella
- 3 tbsp unsweetened cocoa powder
- 3/4 tsp ground cinnamon
- 6 large marshmallows, cut in half

What to do:

1. Preheat your oven to 350 degrees F and line two baking sheets with parchment paper.
2. In a large bowl, break up the cookie dough and add the Nutella, cocoa powder, and cinnamon.
3. Beat with an electric mixer until well mixed.
4. Shape the dough into 12 2-inch balls. Flatten the balls and place half of a large marshmallow in the center of each and fold the dough around the marshmallow.
5. Place the balls 2-inches apart on the baking sheets and bake for 10-12 minutes.
6. Cool on the pan for 5 minutes then transfer to a rack to cool completely before serving.

M&M Cookies

Makes 2 1/2 dozen

What you need:

- 2 ½ cups all-purpose flour
- 2 tsp cornstarch
- 3/4 tsp baking powder
- 1/2 tsp baking soda
- 1 cup butter
- 1 cup brown sugar
- 1/2 cup white sugar
- 1 large egg
- 2 tsp vanilla extract
- 1 11-oz bag M&M's

What to do:

1. Preheat your oven to 375 degrees F and line 2 baking sheets with parchment paper.
2. In a mixing bowl, whisk together the flour, cornstarch, baking powder, baking soda, and salt. Set aside.
3. In a separate mixing bowl, mix together the butter and sugar with an electric mixer until creamy.
4. Mix in the egg and the additional egg yolk.
5. Mix in the vanilla.
6. Slowly mix in the flour mixture until combined.
7. Stir in the M&M's with a spoon, reserve 1/4 cup of M&M's for the tops of the cookies.

8. Scoop out 2 tbsp of dough at a time and form into a balls then place on the prepared baking sheet 2 inches apart.
9. Bake for 10-12 minutes until the edges are golden.
10. Allow the cookies to cool on the baking sheet for 5 minutes then transfer to a wire rack to cool completely.

Martha Washingtons

Makes 24

What you need:

- · 2 cups shredded coconut
- · 8 cups powdered sugar
- · 1 stick butter, melted
- · 1 can sweetened condensed milk
- · 1 tsp vanilla
- · 4 cups chopped pecans
- · Chocolate almond bark

What to do:

1. Combine the coconut, powdered sugar, butter, sweetened condensed milk, vanilla, and pecans in a large bowl.
2. Roll the mixture into small balls and let them chill in the refrigerator for at least 30 minutes.
3. Melt the chocolate and dip the chilled balls into the chocolate, coating well.
4. Allow the chocolate covered balls to cool on parchment paper.

MonKeY BreaD

Servings: 10

What you need:

- 1 16-oz roll of refrigerated biscuits
- 1/2 cup sugar
- 1/2 cup brown sugar
- 1 tsp cinnamon
- 1 stick butter, melted
- 4-oz cream cheese, cubed and softened

What to do:

1. Spray the inside of your slow cooker with non-stick spray.
2. Combine the sugar, brown sugar, and cinnamon in a gallon zip lock bag and set aside.
3. Cut each biscuit into 6 pieces.
4. Dip each biscuit piece into the melted butter.
5. Place dipped biscuits into the gallon zip lock bag with the sugar mixture and shake well to coat.
6. Pour any remaining butter into your slow cooker.
7. Transfer all biscuit pieces to your slow cooker.
8. Cook on low for 2-3 hours or until dough is done.
9. Stir in cubed cream cheese before serving.

Old Fashioned Chocolate Fudge

Makes 36 squares

What you need:

- 2 cups white sugar
- ½ cup cocoa
- 1 cup milk
- 4 tbsp butter
- 1 tsp vanilla extract

What to do:

1. Line a 9x9-inch square baking pan with parchment paper and grease.
2. In a medium saucepan, combine the sugar, cocoa, and milk. Stir to mix together well and bring it to a boil while constantly stirring. Reduce heat to low.
3. Cook, without stirring, until a candy thermometer reaches 238 degrees F.
4. Remove from the heat. Add in the butter and vanilla extract. Stir very well with a wooden spoon.
5. Pour the fudge into the prepared pan and let cool for one hour.
6. Place the baking pan in the refrigerator and let set for 3-4 hours.

oreo Balls

Servings: 24

What you need:

- 15.5-oz package of Oreos
- 8-oz of cream cheese, softened
- 3/4-lb vanilla almond bark, chopped
- Christmas colored sprinkles

What to do:

1. Line a baking sheet with parchment paper.
2. Place the Oreos in a food processor and pulse until finely chopped.
3. Place the chopped Oreos in a large bowl and add in the cream cheese. Mix well.
4. Roll the mixture into 24 balls and place on the prepared baking sheet.
5. Place the baking sheet into your refrigerator for at least 30 minutes or until the balls are firm.
6. In a microwave safe bowl, melt the almond bark in the microwave for 2 minutes, stirring every 30 seconds.
7. Place a skewer or toothpick into the Oreo balls and dip into the melted almond bark until coated.
8. Cover the balls with sprinkles and place back onto the baking sheet.
9. Let the balls cool for at least 30 minutes before serving.

Oreo Peppermint Bark

Servings: 15

What you need:

- · 10 mini candy canes, crushed
- · 12 Oreos, chopped
- · 1 cup chocolate chips
- · 1 1/2 cups white chocolate chips

What to do:

1. Line a baking sheet with parchment paper and spray with non-stick spray.
2. Add the milk chocolate chips to a microwave safe bowl and microwave for 30 second intervals until smooth and melted. Stir between every 30 second interval.
3. Pour the melted chocolate onto the prepared pan and spread it evenly.
4. Sprinkle the chopped Oreos on the warm chocolate and chill for 10 minutes.
5. Add the white chocolate to a microwave safe bowl and microwave for 30 second intervals until smooth and melted. Stir between every interval.
6. Pour the melted white chocolate over the Oreos and spread evenly.
7. Sprinkle the chopped candy canes over the warm white chocolate.
8. Chill until completely set then break into pieces.

oreo peppermint cookies

Makes 36 cookies

What you need:

- 1 box white cake mix
- 1 stick butter, melted
- 1 egg
- 1/2 tsp peppermint extract
- 1/2 tsp vanilla extract
- 4-oz cream cheese, softened and cubed
- 1 cup crushed Oreos
- 1 cup Andes Peppermint Crunch pieces
- 1/2 cup chocolate chips

What to do:

1. In a mixing bowl, combine the cake mix, melted butter, egg, peppermint extract, and vanilla extract. Beat until a dough forms.
2. Add the cream cheese to the dough and mix until combined.
3. Stir in the peppermint crunch pieces and chocolate chips.
4. Stir in the crushed Oreos gently.
5. Refrigerate the dough for 30 minutes.
6. Preheat your oven to 350 degrees F and line a baking sheet or two with parchment paper and spray with non-stick spray.
7. Roll the dough into balls and line them 1-inch apart on the prepared pans.
8. Bake for 9-10 minutes.

9. Remove the pans from the oven and let the cookies sit for 2 minutes before transferring to a wire rack or a sheet of wax paper to cool completely.

peanut Butter Truffles

Makes 35-40

What you need:

- 16-oz Nutter Butter Cookies
- 8-oz cream cheese
- 8-oz Reese's Mini Peanut Butter Cups, quartered
- 12-oz milk chocolate chips
- 3/4 tbsp shortening
- Christmas colored sprinkles

What to do:

1. In a food processor, blend the Nutter Butters into fine crumbs.
2. Cube the cream cheese and place the cubes in the food processor and blend in with the Nutter Butter crumbs.
3. Transfer this mixture to a large bowl.
4. Fold the quartered Reese's cups into the mixture.
5. Roll the mixture into 1-inch balls and place on a sheet of parchment or wax paper on a baking sheet.
6. Freeze for about an hour.
7. Melt the chocolate chips and shortening in a microwave safe bowl in the microwave for 2-3 minutes, stirring every 30 seconds.
8. Dip the frozen balls into the melted chocolate.
9. Place the dipped balls back on the baking sheet to dry.
10. Add the sprinkles before the chocolate dries completely.

peppermint Bark

Servings: 12

What you need:

- 12-oz semi-sweet chocolate chips
- 12-oz white chocolate chips
- 1 tsp peppermint extract
- 1/2 cup crushed peppermints

What to do:

1. Line a baking sheet with parchment paper and spray with non-stick spray.
2. Place the semi-sweet chocolate chips in a microwave safe bowl for 2 minutes, stirring every 30 seconds.
3. Pour the melted chocolate onto the prepared pan and spread into an even layer. Let cool.
4. Repeat step 2 with the white chocolate chips then stir in the peppermint extract.
5. Spread this mixture onto the cooled chocolate layer on the baking sheet.
6. Sprinkle the crushed peppermints onto the white chocolate layer and gently press the pieces in with a spatula.
7. Let cool then break into pieces before serving.

peppermint Brownies

Servings: 8-10

What you need:

- Your favorite boxed brownie mix plus ingredients the directions call for
- 1/2 cup green and red chocolate morsels
- 8-oz cream cheese
- 1/3 cup butter, softened
- 1/2 cup powdered sugar
- 12 peppermint Hershey's Kisses, chopped
- 1/4 tsp peppermint extract
- 3 candy canes, crushed
- Chocolate sauce

What to do:

1. Mix together your brownie mix according to box directions and stir in the 1/2 cup green and red chocolate morsels.
2. While the brownies are baking and cooling, beat the cream cheese and butter in a large bowl with a mixer until creamy and smooth.
3. Gradually add the powdered sugar and mix until smooth.
4. Mix in the peppermint extract.
5. Stir in the chopped Hershey's Kisses.
6. Spread the frosting over the cooled brownies.
7. Sprinkle the crushed candy canes over the frosting.
8. Drizzle on the chocolate sauce.

9. Cut into squares and serve.

peppermint cookies

Makes 3 dozen

What you need:

- 1 1/2 cups powdered sugar
- 1 cup butter, softened
- 1 tsp peppermint extract
- 1 tsp vanilla extract
- 1 egg
- 3 cups flour
- 3 candy canes, crushed
- 1 tsp baking powder
- 1 tsp salt
- 1/2 cup chopped peppermint Hershey's Kisses
- Sugar
- 36 peppermint Hershey's Kisses

What to do:

1. Preheat you oven to 350 degrees F.
2. Line 2 baking sheets with parchment paper and spray with non-stick spray.
3. In a large bowl, mix the powdered sugar, butter, vanilla extract, peppermint extract, and egg with an electric mixer until fluffy.
4. In a separate bowl, combine the flour, crushed candy canes, baking powder, and salt.

5. Add the flour mixture to the wet mixture and mix until well blended.
6. Stir in the chopped Hershey's Kisses.
7. Place about 1/4 cup – 1/2 cup of sugar in a small bowl.
8. Shape the dough into 1-inch balls and roll into the sugar.
9. Place the dough balls on the prepared baking sheets 1-inch apart.
10. Bake for 10-12 minutes or until set.
11. Remove the cookies from the oven and let them cool for 5 minutes then press a Hershey's Kiss in the center of each cookie.

peppermint crunch fudge

Servings: 20

What you need:

- 1 bag peppermint Hershey's Kisses, unwrapped and chopped
- 1/2 cup Andes Peppermint Crunch bites
- 1 cup sugar
- 1/2 cup heavy cream
- 1/2 tsp salt
- 1/2 cup butter
- 1 bag white chocolate chips
- 7-oz marshmallow fluff

What to do:

1. Line a 9x9-inch baking dish with parchment paper.
2. In a large saucepan over medium heat, melt together the sugar, heavy cream, salt, and butter. Bring it to a boil and cook for 5 minutes.
3. Place the white chocolate chips and marshmallow fluff in a large glass bowl.
4. Pour the boiling sugar mixture into the bowl with the chocolate chips and marshmallow fluff and mix with a mixer until smooth.
5. Fold in 3/4 of the chopped Kisses.
6. Pour the mixture into the prepared pan.
7. Sprinkle the rest of the kisses and the Andes Bits on top of the fudge.

8. Refrigerate for a couple hours or until set.
9. Cut into squares and serve or store in an airtight container.

peppermint Dipped oreos

Servings: 10-12

What you need:

- 1 package Oreos
- 1 package vanilla candy melts
- 1 package peppermint baking chips
- Crushed soft peppermints

What to do:

1. In a microwave safe bowl, combine the vanilla candy melts and the peppermint baking chips for 3 minutes, stirring every 30 seconds.
2. Dip each Oreo into the melted mixture then sprinkle with crushed peppermints.
3. Let cool on a sheet of wax paper before serving.

peppermint kiss cookies

Makes: 2 1/2 dozen

What you need:

- 1 1/2 cups powdered sugar
- 1 1/4 cups butter, softened
- 1 tsp peppermint extract
- 1 tsp vanilla extract
- 1 large egg
- 3 cups all-purpose flour
- 1 tsp baking powder
- 1/2 tsp salt
- 1/2 cup finely chopped candy cane flavored Hershey's Kisses
- Granulated sugar
- Additional unwrapped Candy Cane Hershey's Kisses

What to do:

1. Preheat your oven to 350 degrees F and line a baking sheet with parchment paper.
2. In a mixing bowl, mix together the powdered sugar, butter, peppermint extract, vanilla extract, and egg with an electric mixer until creamy.
3. In a separate bowl, whisk together the flour, baking powder, and salt.
4. Slowly add the flour mixture to the sugar/butter mixture until combined.
5. Stir in the chopped Kisses with a spoon.

6. Shape the dough into 1-inch balls and roll in granulated sugar. Place the balls 1-inch apart on the prepared sheet.
7. Bake for 10-12 minutes or until slightly golden.
8. Let the cookies cool for 2-3 minutes on the baking sheet then press a Hershey's Kiss into each cookie.
9. Place the baking sheet in the refrigerator or freezer immediately so that the Kisses don't melt. Leave them in there for 5-10 minutes.
10. Serve or store in an airtight container.

peppermint Meltaway Cookies

Makes about 3 dozen

What you need:

- 1 cup butter, at room temperature
- 1/2 cup powdered sugar
- 1/2 tsp peppermint extract
- 1 1/4 cup all-purpose flour
- 1/2 cup cornstarch
- 2 tbsp butter, softened
- 1 1/2 cups powdered sugar
- 2 tbsp milk
- 1/4 tsp peppermint extract
- 1/2 cup crushed soft peppermints

What to do:

1. Line 2 baking sheets with parchment paper and preheat your oven to 350 degrees F.
2. In a mixing bowl, cream together 1 cup of butter and 1/2 cup powdered sugar until fluffy.
3. Add in the peppermint extract.
4. In a separate bowl, mix together the flour and cornstarch and gradually add it to the butter/sugar mixture and mix well, making a dough.

5. Shape the dough into 1-inch balls. Place them 2 inches apart on the prepared baking sheets.
6. Bake for 10-12 minutes or until the bottoms are light brown.
7. Let the cookies cool on the baking sheets for 5 minutes then transfer to a wire rack to cool completely.
8. In a small bowl, beat 2 tbsp butter, 1 1/2 cups powdered sugar, 2 tbsp milk, and 1/4 tsp peppermint extract. Mix until smooth, making the icing.
9. Spread the icing over the cooled cookies and sprinkle with crushed peppermints.

peppermint patties

Servings: 12

What you need:

- 1/4 cup butter, softened
- 1/3 cup corn syrup
- 4 cups powdered sugar
- 1-2 tsp peppermint extract
- Green and red food coloring
- 12 cup sugar

What to do:

1. In a mixing bowl, combine the softened butter and the corn syrup.
2. Add the 2 cups of powdered sugar and peppermint extract and beat until fully combined.
3. Stir in another cup of powdered sugar.
4. Pour the mixture out onto a cutting board and sprinkle it with the last cup of powdered sugar.
5. Knead the mixture until smooth.
6. Divide the dough into 3 portions.
7. Color one portion with red food coloring and one with green food coloring. I made a well into each portion and filled the well with food coloring then folded and kneaded so it wasn't as messy.
8. Shape the portions into 3/4-inch balls and roll the balls in the sugar.

9. Flatten the balls with a fork.
10. Refrigerate for 3-4 hours before serving or place in an airtight container.

peppermint popcorn Bark

Servings: 18

What you need:

- 2 bags popped popcorn
- 6-oz of candy canes, crushed
- 1 package of white almond bark
- 1 tsp peppermint extract

What to do:

1. Place the popcorn in a very large bowl.
2. Pour the crushed candy canes on top of the popcorn.
3. Melt the almond bark according to the package instructions.
4. Add the peppermint extract to the melted almond bark and stir well.
5. Pour the melted almond bark over the popcorn and stir until the popcorn is coated.
6. Pour the coated popcorn onto wax paper and spread in an even layer.
7. Allow the popcorn to harden then break it into pieces.

peppermint puppy chow

Servings: 10-12

What you need:

- 6-7 cups Chex cereal
- 2 cups white chocolate chips
- 1 tsp vegetable oil
- 1 3/4 cups crushed candy canes
- Powdered sugar

What to do:

1. Place the cereal in a large bowl.
2. In a microwave safe bowl, microwave the white chocolate chips and vegetable oil at 30 seconds intervals until melted and smooth. Stir between each interval.
3. Pour the melted chocolate over the cereal and stir to coat well.
4. Pour the mixture into a large ziplock bag.
5. Place the crushed candy canes and about 2 cups of powdered sugar in the bag. Close the bag and shake well to coat. Add more powdered sugar if you want!

peppermint Rice krispie Treats

Servings: 10-12

What you need:

- · 10 1/2-oz bag of peppermint mini marshmallows
- · 1/4 cup butter
- · 5 cups rice krispie cereal
- · 1/4 cup semi-sweet chocolate chips
- · 1/4 cup white chocolate chips
- · 1/2 tsp vegetable oil
- · 1/8 tsp peppermint extract
- · 3 medium sized candy canes, crushed

What to do:

1. Line a 9x13-inch pan with foil and spray with non-stick spray.
2. Melt the butter in a large bowl in the microwave.
3. Add the marshmallows to the bowl and stir well.
4. Heat at 30 seconds intervals until the marshmallows are melted and smooth. Stir between each interval.
5. Add the Rice Krispies to the bowl and stir to combine.
6. Press the mixture into the prepared pan.
7. In a microwave safe bowl, combine the white chocolate chips and 1/4 tsp vegetable oil. Heat in the microwave until melted and smooth, stirring every 30 seconds.

8. Sprinkle the melted white chocolate over the rice krispie treats.
9. In a microwave safe bowl, combine the semi-sweet chocolate chips, 1/4 tsp vegetable oil, and the peppermint extract. Microwave until melted and smooth, stirring every 30 seconds.
10. Drizzle the chocolate over the Rice Krispies.
11. Sprinkle the crushed candy canes on top and let sit until the chocolate is set before cutting into squares and serving.

peppermint sticks

Makes 16

What you need:

- 4-oz semisweet chocolate chips
- 1 tsp shortening
- 2/3 cup toasted pecans, chopped
- 16 3-inch soft peppermint sticks

What to do:

1. In a small saucepan over low heat, combine the chocolate chips and shortening. Cook until melted.
2. Transfer the melted chocolate to a bowl.
3. Place the pecans in a shallow dish.
4. Dip each peppermint stick into the melted chocolate then coat with crushed pecans.
5. Place on wax paper and let cool.

Pumpkin Bars

Servings: 8-10

What you need:

· 2 cups flour
· 2 tsp baking powder
· 2 tsp cinnamon
· 1/2 tsp nutmeg
· 1 tsp salt
· 1 tsp baking soda
· 4 eggs
· 1 2/3 cup sugar
· 1 cup oil
· 1 15-oz can pumpkin
· 8-oz cream cheese, softened
· 1/3 cup butter
· 3 cups powdered sugar
· 1 cup whipped cream
· 1 tbsp milk

What to do:

1. Preheat your oven to 350 degrees F and grease a 15x10 baking pan.
2. In a small bowl, sift together the flour, baking powder, cinnamon, nutmeg, salt, and baking soda.
3. In a large mixing bowl, combine the eggs, sugar, oil, and pumpkin until mixed well.

4. Gradually mix in the dry ingredients and mix well.
5. Spread the batter into the baking dish and bake for 25-30 minutes or until a toothpick inserted into the center comes out clean.
6. While the bars are in the oven, place the cream cheese and butter in a mixing bowl and cream together.
7. Add in the powdered sugar, whipped cream, vanilla extract, and milk. Mix until fluffy.
8. Place the frosting in the refrigerator.
9. When the bars are finished cooking, let them cool completely then frost them generously.

Pumpkin Pie

Servings: 6

What you need:

- 1 15-oz can of pumpkin
- 2/3 cup cinnamon bun flavored coffee creamer
- 2 tbsp pumpkin pie spice (divided)
- 1 9-oz yellow cake mix
- 1 cup chopped pecans
- 1/4 cup butter

What to do:

1. Spray the inside of your slow cooker with non-stick spray.
2. In a medium bowl, mix together the pumpkin, coffee creamer, and 1 tbsp of pumpkin pie spice.
3. Spread the mixture into your slow cooker.
4. In a separate bowl, mix together the cake mix, pecans, and 1 tsp pumpkin pie spice.
5. Sprinkle the mixture over the pumpkin mixture in your slow cooker.
6. Drizzle the melted butter over the top of the dry mixture.
7. Cover and cook on high for 2 1/2 hours.
8. Serve warm.

Red Velvet Cookies

Makes 2 dozen

What you need:

- 1 box red velvet cake mix
- 6 tbsp butter, melted
- 1 cup powdered sugar
- 1 tsp cornstarch
- 2 eggs

What to do:

1. Preheat your oven to 375 degrees F and line a baking sheet with parchment paper.
2. Combine the cornstarch and powdered sugar in a small bowl.
3. In a large bowl, combine the cake mix, melted butter, and eggs. Mix on low with an electric mixer.
4. Roll into 1-inch balls and roll in the powdered sugar/cornstarch mixture.
5. Place balls 2-inches apart on the prepared baking sheet.
6. Bake for 9-11 minutes or until set.
7. Let cool on the baking sheets for 5 minutes before transferring to a wire rack to cool completely.

Red Velvet Fudge

Makes 24 squares

What you need:

- 3 cups sugar
- 3/4 cup butter
- 2/3 cup half and half
- 12-oz white chocolate chips
- 7-oz marshmallow cream
- 1 tsp vanilla
- 1 cup semi-sweet chocolate chips
- 3 tbsp red food coloring

What to do:

1. Line a 9x9-inch baking dish with foil, with the ends of the foil extending over the sides. Lightly spray the foil with non-stick spray.
2. In a large glass microwave safe bowl, add the butter and cover with a paper towel. Microwave on high for 1 1/2 minutes.
3. Add the sugar and the half and half to the melted butter and mix well. Microwave for 3 minutes. Stir and cook for another 2 minutes.
4. Stir very well, scrape down the sides, and microwave for another 2 minutes.
5. Add the marshmallow cream and stir.
6. Add the white chocolate chips and vanilla. Stir until everything is very smooth.

7. In a separate microwave bowl, add the semi-sweet chocolate chips and food coloring. Add half of the hot white chocolate mixture into the bowl with the semi-sweet chocolate chips. Stir well.

8. With 2 ice cream scoops, dollop scoops of each mixture into a random pattern into the prepared baking dish.

9. When all of both of the mixtures are in the pan, lift the pan about an inch and drop it on the counter to remove air bubbles. Repeat about 5 times.

10. Run a knife through the fudge mixture to make it swirly.

11. Let the fudge cool completely before lifting it from the dish and cutting into squares.

Reindeer Chow

Servings: 16-18

What you need:

- 14 cups Chex cereal
- 18-oz red and green M&M's
- 12-oz semi-sweet chocolate chips
- 1/2 cup butter
- 1 cup peanut butter
- 1 tsp vanilla extract
- 4-5 cups powdered sugar

What to do:

1. In a microwave safe bowl, melt the peanut butter and butter at 30 second intervals until butter is melted completely.
2. Add the chocolate and stir until they are melted, microwave at 30 second intervals if necessary.
3. Pour half of the Chex cereal into a very large bowl.
4. Drizzle half of the chocolate/peanut butter mixture over the cereal and mix with a spoon.
5. Pour 1 cup of powdered sugar into a gallon zip lock bag and add half of the covered cereal mix. Close the bag and shake until the cereal is coated.
6. Repeat step 5 until all of the coated cereal is covered in powdered sugar.
7. Repeat steps 3-6 until all cereal is covered in powdered sugar.

8. Place all of the cereal in a large container and toss in the M&M's.

Rolo Turtles

Makes 50

What you need:

- 50 checkerboard pretzels
- 50 individual Rolos
- 50 pecan halves, toasted

What to do:

1. Preheat your oven to 350 degrees F.
2. Line a baking sheet with parchment paper.
3. Evenly space the pretzels on the prepared baking sheet.
4. Place one Rolo on each pretzel.
5. Place the baking sheet in the preheated oven for 5 minutes.
6. Remove the baking sheet from the oven and place a pecan on top of each Rolo and carefully press down. Don't burn yourself!

Snicker Doodles

Makes 2 dozen

What you need:

- 1/2 cup shortening
- 3/4 cup granulated sugar
- 1 egg
- 1 tbsp vanilla
- 1 1/2 cups all-purpose flour
- 1/2 tsp baking soda
- 1/4 tsp cream of tartar
- 1 tbsp cinnamon
- 3 tbsp granulated sugar

What to do:

1. Preheat your oven to 350 degrees F and line a baking sheet with parchment paper.
2. Cream together the shortening and sugar in a mixing bowl with an electric mixer.
3. Add the egg and vanilla and mix well.
4. In a separate bowl, combine the flour, baking soda, salt, and cream of tartar and mix well.
5. Slowly add the dry ingredients to the wet ingredients.
6. Roll the dough into 1-inch balls.
7. In a small bowl, mix together 1 tbsp of cinnamon and 3 tbsp of sugar.
8. Roll the dough balls into the cinnamon and sugar mixture.

9. Place the balls on the prepared baking sheet and bake for 9-11 minutes or until edges are golden.
10. Let cool on the baking sheet for 5 minutes before transferring to a wire rack to cool completely.

Snowballs

Makes 64

What you need:

- 12-oz white chocolate chips
- 1/4 cup heavy cream
- 1 1/4 cup slivered almonds, finely ground
- 2 tbsp dark rum
- 1 1/2 cups shredded coconut

What to do:

1. In a double boiler, melt the white chocolate chips with the heavy cream, stirring constantly.
2. Stir in the almonds and the rum.
3. Pour the mixture into a square baking pan and chill for an hour or until firm.
4. Cut into squares and roll each square into a ball.
5. Roll each ball into the coconut.
6. Chill until ready to serve.

sugar cookies

Makes 40-50 cookies

What you need:

- 1 cup unsalted butter, at room temperature
- 1 1/4 cup sugar
- 1 egg
- 1 1/2 tsp vanilla extract
- 1/2 tsp almond extract
- 3 cups flour
- 1 1/2 tsp baking powder
- 1/4 tsp salt
- Colored sugar, sprinkles, or icing-for decorating

What to do:

1. In a large mixing bowl, cream together the butter and sugar until fluffy.
2. Add in the egg, vanilla extract, and almond extract until well combined.
3. In a separate bowl, combine the flour, baking powder, and salt.
4. Slowly add the flour mixture to the butter/sugar mixture and mix well.
5. Roll the dough with a rolling pin between 2 sheets of parchment or wax paper and place on a baking sheet.
6. Refrigerate for 30 minutes.

7. Preheat your oven to 350 degrees F and line 2 baking sheets with parchment paper.
8. Cut the dough into shapes using cookie cutter and transfer to a baking sheet.
9. Sprinkle with colored sugars (if using) and bake for 8-12 minutes.
10. Cool on the baking sheet for 5 minutes then transfer to a rack to cool completely.
11. Store in an airtight container.

Turtle Brownies

Servings: 8-10

What you need:

- Your favorite brownie box mix plus ingredients the directions call for
- 1 tbsp strongly brewed coffee, leftover cold coffee is fine
- 8-oz caramel sauce
- 1 cup chopped pecans
- ½ cup chocolate chips
- ½ cup chopped pecans

What to do:

1. Preheat your oven to 350 degrees F and line an 8-inch square pan with aluminum foil. Let the foil hang over the edges a bit. Spray with non-stick spray.
2. Mix together your boxed brownie mix according to package directions.
3. Add the coffee, caramel sauce, 1 cup of chopped pecans, and chocolate chips to the mix and stir together.
4. Evenly sprinkle the ½ cup chopped pecans over the batter.
5. Bake for 22-25 minutes, or until a toothpick inserted into the center comes out clean.
6. Allow the brownies to cool, then cut them into squares and serve.

White Chocolate Cherry Cookies

Makes about 50 cookies

What you need:

- 1/2 cup maraschino cherries, drained and chopped
- 2 1/2 cups all-purpose flour
- 1/2 cup sugar
- 1 cup butter
- 12-oz white chocolate baking squares, finely chopped
- 1/2 tsp almond extract
- 2 drops red food coloring
- Sugar
- 2 tsp shortening
- Red and white sprinkles

What to do:

1. Preheat your oven to 325 degrees F and line a baking sheet with parchment paper.
2. In a large bowl, stir together the flour and 1/2 cup sugar. Cut in the butter until the mixture is crumbly.
3. Stir in the cherries and 4-oz of white chocolate.
4. Stir in the almond extract and food coloring.
5. Form the mixture into a ball and knead until smooth.
6. Shape the dough into 1-inch balls and place them 2 inches apart on the prepared sheet. Flatten the balls.

7. Bake for 10-12 minutes then let cool on the baking sheet for 2
    minutes.

White Chocolate Cranberry Cookies

Makes about 2 dozen

What you need:

- 3/4 cup unsalted butter, at room temperature
- 3/4 cup brown sugar
- 1/4 cup granulated sugar
- 1 large egg, at room temperature
- 2 tbsp vanilla extract
- 2 cups all-purpose flour
- 2 tsp cornstarch
- 1 tsp baking soda
- 1/2 tsp salt
- 3/4 cup white chocolate chips
- 1/4 cup dried cranberries

What to do:

1. In a large mixing bowl, beat the butter, brown sugar, and granulated sugar with a mixer until smooth and creamy.
2. Add the egg and vanilla and mix together.
3. In a separate bowl, stir together the flour, cornstarch, baking soda, and salt.
4. Slowly mix the flour mixture into the wet mixture until well combined.
5. Stir in the white chocolate chips and dried cranberries.

6. Chill the dough for at least 2 hours.
7. Preheat your oven to 350 degrees F and line a large baking sheet or two with parchment paper.
8. Roll the dough into 1-inch balls and place on the baking sheet(s) 1-2 inches apart.
9. Bake for 8-10 minutes or until golden around the edges.
10. Allow the cookie to cool on the sheet for 5 minutes then transfer to a wire rack to cool.
11. Serve or store in an airtight container.

White Chocolate Peppermint Fudge

Makes 2 lbs

What you need:

- 1 1/2 tsp plus 1/4 cup butter, softened
- 2 cups sugar
- 1/2 cup sour cream
- 12-oz white chocolate baking squares, chopped
- 7-oz marshmallow cream
- 1/2 cup crushed peppermints
- 1/2 tsp peppermint extract

What to do:

1. Line a 9x9-inch baking dish with foil. Grease the foil with 1 1/2 tsp of butter.
2. In a large heavy saucepan over medium heat, combine the sugar, sour cream, and 1/4 cup butter. Stir until the sugar is dissolved then bring to a rapid boil. Stir until a candy thermometer reaches 234 degrees F (about 5 minutes).
3. Remove the saucepan from the heat and stir in the white chocolate and marshmallow cream until they are melted.
4. Fold in the crushed peppermints and peppermint extract.
5. Pour the mixture into the prepared pan.
6. Place the pan in your refrigerator for at least an hour or until firm.

7. Lift the fudge out of the pan and gently peel off the foil.
8. Cut into 1-inch squares.

DRINKS

Almond Joy

Servings: 16

What you need:

· 2 cups corn syrup
· 1 cup sugar
· 1/4 cup butter
· 1/2 tsp salt
· 1 cup chopped roasted almonds
· 14-oz coconut flakes
· 1 tsp almond extract
· 1-lb almond bark, chopped

What to do:

1. Line a baking sheet with parchment paper and spray with non-stick spray.
2. In a heavy saucepan over medium high heat, combine the corn syrup, butter, sugar, and salt and stir until the mixture comes to a boil. Stir until a candy thermometer reaches 230 degrees F then remove from heat.
3. Stir in the nuts, almond extract and coconut.
4. Press the mixture into the prepared pan and let cool.
5. Cut into squares.
6. Melt the almond bark in a microwave safe bowl in the microwave for 3 minutes, stirring every 30 seconds.
7. Drizzle the chocolate over the coconut/almond squares.
8. Let cool then serve.

Andes Mint Hot Chocolate

Servings: 4-5

What you need:

- 1 bag Andes crème de menthe baking chips
- 2 cups Rumchata
- 2 cups half and half
- 2 cups milk
- Marshmallows

What to do:

1. Put all of the ingredients in your slow cooker and cook on high for an hour, stirring occasionally.
2. Turn your slow cooker to low or warm and serve topped with marshmallows.

caramel Apple cider

Servings: 2

What you need:

- 3 tbsp cinnamon Dulce syrup
- 12-oz apple juice or store bought apple cider
- Whipped cream
- Caramel sauce

What to do:

1. Pour the 3 tbsp of cinnamon Dulce syrup in a small saucepan over medium heat.
2. Add 12-oz of apple juice or apple cider to the saucepan and bring to a simmer.
3. Add the cider to a mug and top with whipped cream and caramel sauce.
4. Serve immediately.

caramel apple Hot Toddy

Servings: 8-10

What you need:

- 1 1/2 cups caramel vodka
- 1/2 gallon apple cider
- 1/2 cup bourbon
- 3 cinnamon sticks
- Whipped cream

What to do:

1. In a saucepan over medium-low heat, mix together the vodka, cider, bourbon, and cinnamon sticks until heated through.
2. Ladle into mugs and top with whipped cream before serving.

caramel Apple sangria

Servings: 10-12

What you need:

· 1 750ml bottle of Pinot Grigio
· 1 cup caramel vodka
· 6 cups apple cider
· 2 medium apples, cored and sliced

What to do:

1. Stir the wine, vodka, and apple cider together in a large pitcher or punch bowl.
2. Add the chopped apples to the pitcher or punch bowl.
3. Serve over ice.

caramel Hot Chocolate

Servings: 2

What you need:

- 2 cups whole milk
- 1/2 cup chocolate chips
- 1/2 cup caramel sauce
- Marshmallows
- Grated chocolate, as garnish
- Caramel sauce, for drizzling

What to do:

1. In a medium sauce pan over medium heat, add the milk, chocolate chips, and caramel. Whisk until the chocolate chips are melted.
2. Serve warm topped with marshmallows, grated chocolate, and caramel sauce.

Chocolate Chip Peppermint Milkshake

Servings: 2

What you need:

- 2 cups vanilla ice cream
- 1/2 cup milk
- 1 tsp peppermint extract
- 4 candy canes, crushed
- 1/4 cup chocolate chips
- Whipped cream
- Extra crushed candy canes

What to do:

1. Put the ice cream, milk, peppermint extract, and crushed candy canes in your blender and blend until smooth.
2. Add in the chocolate chips and pulse for a few seconds.
3. Pour into a cup or cups and top with whipped cream and the extra crushed candy canes.

Chocolate Peppermint Protein Shake

Servings: 1

What you need:

- 1 large banana, frozen
- 2-3 large ice cubes
- 1 cup milk
- 1 scoop chocolate protein powder
- 2 tbsp cocoa powder
- Pinch of sea salt
- 1/4 tsp peppermint extract
- 1 tbsp dark chocolate chips
- Whipped cream

What to do:

1. Place all of the ingredients except the whipped cream in your blender and blend until smooth.
2. Pour into a glass and top with whipped cream.

cookies and cream Hot chocolate

Servings: 2

What you need:

- 2 cups milk
- 1/2 cup hot chocolate powder
- 1/2 cup Bailey's Irish Cream
- 5 Oreos, finely crushed
- Whipped cream
- Extra crushed Oreos for topping

What to do:

1. Heat the milk in a medium saucepan over medium heat but don't let it boil.
2. When the milk is simmering, add the hot chocolate powder.
3. Add the crushed Oreos to the milk.
4. Remove from the heat and stir in the Bailey's.
5. Serve in a mug topped with whipped cream and crushed Oreos.

cranberry Mimosa

Servings: 20+

What you need:

- 1 bottle cranberry juice
- 1 bottle sparkling white wine

What to do:

1. Mix the cranberry juice and sparkling wine together and pour into champagne glasses.
2. Serve!

Slow Cooker Apple Cider

Servings: 20+

What you need:

- 2 quarts store bought apple cider
- 1/4 cup brown sugar
- 1/8 tsp ground ginger
- 1 orange, unpeeled and cut into wedges
- 2 cinnamon sticks
- 1 tsp whole cloves
- Cheesecloth

What to do:

1. Tie up the cinnamon sticks and whole cloves in the cheesecloth.
2. Add all of the ingredients to your slow cooker.
3. Cover and cook on low for 3 hours.
4. Remove the cheesecloth bag and the orange wedges before serving.
5. Store any leftovers in the refrigerator and reheat before serving.

Slow Cooker Creamy Hot Chocolate

Servings: 8-10

What you need:

- · 14-oz can of sweetened condensed milk
- · 1 1/2 cups heavy whipping cream
- · 6 cups milk
- · 1 1/2 tsp vanilla
- · 2 cups chocolate chips

What to do:

1. Pour all of the ingredients into your slow cooker and stir together well.
2. Cover and cook on low for 2 hours, stirring occasionally.
3. Serve topped with marshmallows.

Slow Cooker Mint Hot Chocolate

Servings: 16

What you need:

- 1 gallon of milk
- 20 mini peppermint patties, chopped
- 1 1/2 cups hot chocolate powder
- 1 tbsp vanilla
- Whipped cream
- Chocolate syrup

What to do:

1. Add all of the ingredients to your slow cooker, except the whipped cream and chocolate syrup.
2. Heat on low for 2 hours, stirring occasionally.
3. Vigorously beat with a whisk to make the hot chocolate light and frothy.
4. Pour into mugs and top with whipped cream and chocolate syrup.

DirtY SanTa

Servings: 1

What you need:

- 4-oz coffee, frozen into ice cubes
- 4-oz Bailey's Irish Cream
- 1-oz vanilla vodka

What to do:

1. Place the coffee ice cubes in a glass.
2. Pour the Bailey's and vodka in a shaker and strain over the ice.
3. Serve!

Easy Pumpkin Spice Latte

Servings: 2

What you need:

- 1/2 cup pumpkin puree
- 1 cup French vanilla liquid coffee creamer
- 2 tsp pumpkin pie spice
- 1 1/2 cups hot strong coffee
- Whipped cream
- Cinnamon

What to do:

1. In a medium saucepan over medium heat, whisk together the pumpkin puree, coffee creamer, and pumpkin pie spice until smooth.
2. Reduce the heat to low and simmer for 5 minutes.
3. Pour in the coffee.
4. Pour into coffee mugs and top with whipped cream and cinnamon.
5. Serve immediately.

Eggnog

Servings: 3-4

What you need:

- 6 large egg yolks
- 1/2 cup sugar
- 1 cup heavy cream
- 2 cups milk
- 1 1/2 tsp freshly grated nutmeg
- A pinch of salt
- 1/4 tsp vanilla extract
- 1/8 tsp rum extract

What to do:

1. In a large bowl, whisk together the egg yolks and sugar until creamy.
2. In a large saucepan over medium heat, stir together the heavy cream, milk, nutmeg and salt and bring to a simmer. Stir often.
3. Ladle 1/2 cup of the cream/milk mixture into the egg mixture and whisk vigorously.
4. Ladle in another 1/2 cup of the cream/milk mixture and whisk vigorously. Repeat until all of the cream/milk mixture has been added to the egg mixture.
5. Pour the mixture back into the saucepan over medium heat and continuously whisk until it reaches 160 degrees F on a thermometer.

6. Remove from the heat and stir in the vanilla extract and rum extract.
7. Pour into a pitcher or bowl and refrigerate until chilled.

Gingerbread Martini

Servings: 1

What you need:

- 1 1/2-oz vodka
- 1/2-oz brandy
- 2-oz coffee-mate gingerbread latte
- Cinnamon, as garnish

What to do:

1. Shake all of the ingredients together in a shaker and strain into a chilled martini glass.
2. Garnish with cinnamon and serve.

Grinch Punch

Servings: 16

What you need:

- 1/3 cup sugar
- 1/3 cup water
- 1/3 cup evaporated milk
- 1/2 tsp almond extract
- 12 drops neon green food coloring
- 2 liters lemon lime soda
- 1 pint vanilla ice cream
- 1 pint lime sherbet

What to do:

1. In a large saucepan over medium heat, combine the sugar and water and heat until the sugar is dissolved.
2. Remove the saucepan from the heat and stir in the evaporated milk and almond extract. Cover and refrigerate until chilled.
3. Pour the milk mixture into a large punch bowl. Stir in the food coloring and the lemon-lime soda.
4. Top with the vanilla ice cream and lime sherbet and serve.

Holiday Sangria

Servings: 20+

What you need:

- 1 bottle white wine
- 1 bottle sparkling cider
- 2 oranges, sliced
- 1 red apple, cored and chopped
- 1 green apple, cored and chopped
- 2 cups cranberries

What to do:

1. Combine the wine and cider in a pitcher.
2. Add all of the fruit.
3. Stir well and chill until ready to serve.

Holiday White Wine Spritzer

Servings: 20+

What you need:

- 1.5 L of Barefoot Moscato White Wine
- 1 L of diet sprite
- 1 L of red cream soda
- 12-oz of frozen raspberries

What to do:

1. Pour the wine, sprite, and cream soda in a large pitcher or punch bowl.
2. Add the frozen raspberries and serve.

Hot Buttered Rum

Servings: 4

What you need:

- 2 cups water
- 1/2 stick butter
- 1/4 cup packed brown sugar
- 1 tsp cinnamon
- 1/2 tsp freshly grated nutmeg
- 1/4 tsp ground cloves
- 1/8 tsp salt
- 2/3 cup dark rum

What to do:

1. In a medium saucepan over medium-high heat, bring the water, butter, brown sugar, cinnamon, nutmeg, cloves, and salt to a boil.
2. Reduce heat and simmer, stirring occasionally, for 10 minutes.
3. Remove from the heat, stir in the rum, and serve.

Kahlua Hot Chocolate

Servings: 2

What you need:

- 2 cups whole milk
- 1/2 cup chocolate sauce
- 4-oz Kahlua
- Whipped cream
- Extra chocolate sauce for drizzling

What to do:

1. In a medium saucepan over medium heat, combine the milk and chocolate sauce. Bring to a simmer.
2. Remove from heat and stir in the Kahlua.
3. Transfer to mugs and top with whipped cream and drizzle with chocolate sauce.

Mocha peppermint Frappe

Servings: 1-2

What you need:

- 1 1/2 cups strong brewed coffee, partially frozen
- 1/2 cup milk
- 2 tsp unsweetened cocoa powder
- 1 tsp stevia (or to taste)
- 1/2 tsp peppermint extract
- Whipped cream
- Crushed peppermints

What to do:

1. In your blender, combine the coffee, milk, cocoa powder, stevia, and peppermint extract until smooth.
2. Pour into a glass and top with whipped cream and crushed peppermints.

Nutella Hot Chocolate

Servings: 4-6

What you need:

- 5 cups milk
- 1/2 cup cocoa powder
- 1/2 cup Nutella
- 1/2 cup sugar
- 1 cup water

What to do:

1. Combine the cocoa, Nutella, sugar, and water in a large pan on your stove. Stir and bring to a gentle boil until the sugar and cocoa are dissolved.
2. Pour the mixture into your slow cooker.
3. Add the milk to your slow cooker and stir.
4. Cook on high for 2 hours or on low for 4 hours.
5. Pour into mugs and serve.

peppermint Eggnog

Servings: 6-8

What you need:

- 1 quart eggnog
- 3/4 cup white chocolate chips
- 1/3 cup crushed candy canes
- Whipped cream
- Extra crushed candy canes

What to do:

1. In a saucepan over medium heat, combine the eggnog, white chocolate chips, and crushed candy canes in a saucepan. Stir occasionally and heat until the white chocolate is melted.
2. Pour into mugs and top with whipped cream and crushed candy canes.

Peppermint Hot Chocolate

Servings: 4-6

What you need:

- 5 cups milk
- 1/2 cup cocoa powder
- 1/2 cup sugar
- 1 cup water
- 4 tsp peppermint syrup

What to do:

1. Combine the cocoa, sugar, and water in a large pan on your stove. Stir and bring to a gentle boil until the sugar and cocoa are dissolved.
2. Pour the mixture into your slow cooker.
3. Add the milk and peppermint syrup to your slow cooker and stir.
4. Cook on high for 2 hours or on low for 4 hours.
5. Pour into mugs and serve.

Peppermint Milkshake

Servings: 1-2

What you need:

- 3 large scoops of vanilla bean ice cream
- 1/2 tsp peppermint extract
- 3/4 cup milk
- Whipped cream
- 1 candy cane, crushed

What to do:

1. In a blender, blend the ice cream, milk, and peppermint extract.
2. Top with whipped cream and crushed candy canes.

peppermint mocha

Servings: 1

What you need:

- 1/4 cup sugar
- 1/4 cup water
- 1/4 tsp peppermint extract
- 3 tbsp powdered cocoa
- 3 tbsp hot water
- 1/2 cup hot espresso or strong brewed coffee
- 1 1/2 cup steamed milk
- Whipped cream

What to do:

1. In a small saucepan over medium heat, stir together the water and sugar. Bring to a boil and let the sugar dissolve. Reduce heat to a simmer and add the peppermint extract. Let simmer for 20 minutes.
2. Mix the cocoa and 3 tbsp of hot water in a mug until a paste forms.
3. Add the espresso and the sugar/water/peppermint mixture to the mug and stir well.
4. Add the milk, stir, and serve.
5. Top with whipped cream.

Pumpkin Pie White Hot Chocolate

Servings: 2

What you need:

- · 2 cups milk
- · 1/2 cup white chocolate chips
- · 2 tbsp canned pumpkin
- · 1 tbsp corn starch
- · 1 tbsp vanilla extract
- · Marshmallows

What to do:

1. In a medium saucepan over low heat, add the milk, chocolate chips, pumpkin, corn starch, and vanilla extract.
2. Whisk together until combined and let simmer for 5-7 minutes or until chocolate is melted and liquid is thickened.
3. Pour into two coffee mugs.
4. Top with marshmallows before serving.

Red Velvet Hot Chocolate

Servings: 4

What you need:

- 4 cups whole milk
- 1/4 cup sugar
- 10-oz chocolate chips
- 2 tsp red food coloring
- 1 tsp vanilla extract
- Whipped cream

What to do:

1. In a medium saucepan over medium heat, add the milk and sugar and stir until the sugar is dissolved and the mixture is heated thoroughly.
2. Remove from the heat and stir in the chocolate until it is melted. Stir in the food coloring and vanilla extract.
3. Pour the mixture into mugs and top with whipped cream.

Spiced White Chocolate Cocoa

Servings: 12

What you need:

- · 16-oz good quality white chocolate, chopped
- · 4 cups milk
- · 4 cups heavy cream
- · 1 tbsp vanilla extract
- · 1/4 tsp ground nutmeg
- · 3 cinnamon sticks
- · Whipped cream

What to do:

1. Place the white chocolate in the bottom of your slow cooker.
2. Add all the remaining ingredients except the whipped cream to the slow cooker and stir.
3. Cook on low for 2 hours, stirring occasionally.
4. Ladle into mugs and top with whipped cream to serve.

S'mores Hot Chocolate

Servings: 2-3

What you need:

- 3 cups milk
- 1/4 cup cocoa powder
- 2 tbsp chocolate syrup
- 2-3 tbsp sugar
- A pinch of salt
- Crushed graham crackers
- 1/2 cup marshmallows

What to do:

1. Preheat your oven to low broil and place a rack in the second to the highest position. Place a baking sheet on the rack.
2. In a saucepan over medium heat, heat the milk until warm but do not boil.
3. When milk is simmering, add the cocoa powder, chocolate syrup, sugar, and salt. Whisk vigorously.
4. Pour the hot chocolate into glass mugs.
5. Top the hot chocolate with 1/4 cup of marshmallows each.
6. Carefully place the mugs on the baking sheet in the oven and broil until the marshmallows are browned but not burned! Watch them carefully.
7. Carefully remove the mugs from the oven and sprinkle crushed graham crackers over the marshmallows.

Spiced Eggnog

Makes about 1 quart

What you need:

- 1 quart store-bought eggnog
- 1/4 cup spiced rum
- 1/4 cup Kahlua
- 2 tbsp bourbon
- 1/2 tsp vanilla extract
- Ground cinnamon
- Ground cloves
- Ground nutmeg
- Brown sugar

What to do:

1. Place the eggnog, rum, Kahlua, bourbon, and vanilla in your blender and pulse for a few seconds.
2. Rim glasses with brown sugar.
3. Pour eggnog into each glass.
4. Sprinkle eggnog with cinnamon, cloves, and nutmeg.
5. Serve!

White peppermint Hot Chocolate

Servings: 4

What you need:

· 2/3 cup heavy whipping cream
· 8 peppermints, crushed
· 4 cups milk
· 8-oz white chocolate, chopped
· 1/2 tsp peppermint extract
· Crushed peppermints, for garnish

What to do:

1. In a medium bowl with a mixer, beat the heavy whipping cream and crushed peppermints until stiff peaks form. Cover and refrigerate.
2. In a large saucepan, heat the milk over medium heat.
3. Add the white chocolate to the milk and whisk until it is melted completely.
4. Stir in the peppermint extract.
5. Ladle the hot chocolate into mugs and top with the whipped cream mixture from the refrigerator.
6. Top the whipped cream with crushed peppermints and serve.

The Grinch

Servings: 1

What you need:

- 1 large scoop of lime sherbet
- 1 cup of ginger ale
- 2-oz whipped cream vodka or regular vodka
- Green decorating sugar

What to do:

1. Rim a tall glass with green decorating sugar.
2. In your blender, mix together the sherbet, ginger ale, and vodka.
3. Pour into the glass and serve.

YOU WILL ALSO ENJOY

WWW.HANNIEPSCOTT.COM/BOOKS

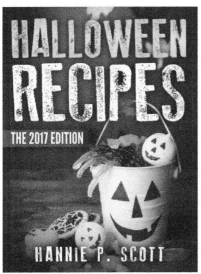

ABOUT THE AUTHOR

Hannie P. Scott, Full-Time Mom and Food Blogger

Driven by her desire for cooking for others (and herself), Hannie spends a lot of time in the kitchen! She enjoys sharing her love of food with the world by creating "no-nonsense" recipe books that anyone can use to make delicious meals.

Hannie attended the University of Southern Mississippi and received a Bachelor's degree in Nutrition & Dietetics. She enjoys cooking and experimenting with food. She hopes to inspire readers and help them build confidence in their cooking. All Hannie's recipes are easy-to-prepare with easy-to-acquire ingredients.

For more recipes, cooking tips, and Hannie's blog, visit:

www.HanniePScott.com

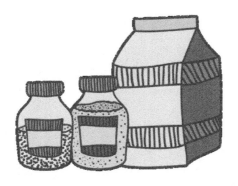

NOTES

NOTES

NOTES

NOTES

NOTES

NOTES